THE WOODLAND INDIANS

C. Keith Wilbur's Illustrated Living History Series

The Illustrated Living History Series

THE WOODLAND INDIANS

by

C. Keith Wilbur

The
Globe
Pequot
Press

Guilford, Connecticut

Library of Congress Cataloging-in-Publication Data

Wilbur, C. Keith.
    The Woodland Indians / by C. Keith Wilbur. — 1st ed.
     p. cm. — (The illustrated living history series)
    Includes bibliographical references.
    ISBN 1-56440-625-3
    1. Woodland Indians—History—Juvenile literature. 2. Woodland
Indians—Social life and customs—Juvenile literature. I. Title
II. Series
E78.E2W55 1995
973'.04973—dc20
                                   95-3098
                                   CIP

Manufactured in the United States of America
First Edition/Seventh Printing

CONTENTS

PREFACE

There are those special moments in a lifetime when a ho-hum day unexpectedly is filled with excitement and wonder. It was one such lazy summer's day when I was a child, that found me skimming disc-shaped stones over the waters of Narragansett Bay. I was about to try topping my seven-skip record when the flattish, sharp-ended stone in my hand demanded a second look. An Indian arrowhead! Eight year olds have vivid imaginations, and I put mine to use picturing the Rhode Island warrior who might have zeroed in on a deer or bear on that very spot. That moment marked the beginning of my abiding interest in our local Narragansett and Wampanoag tribes that soon extended to their New England neighbors.

I hadn't realized that the tribes who had lived almost in my own Cranston backyard were really a part of a much broader picture. While they shared many traditions with the other early Americans of the United States, there were surprising differences between the Algonquians, the Iroquois, and the southeastern tribes. The interrelationships of these woodland peoples have long been lost in misunderstandings and uncertainties. Fortunately, improving dating methods, new discoveries, and exacting research have recently answered many of our puzzlements.

Perhaps you've wondered when the bow and arrow came into its own, why the Ohio Mound Builders built their earthen monuments, and why the southeastern tribes had Mayan-like temple mounds and followed the curious practice of skinning corpses, how the "Red Paint People" came by their name, and the reasons why prisoner sacrifice and cannibalism became part of the southeastern Indian and Iroquoian warfare. These and other questions are answered in the following pages — and finding an arrowhead is not a prerequisite for understanding the prehistoric American Woodland Indians.

INTRODUCTION: THE FIRST FOOTPRINTS

High on the list of the world's great adventures must be the exploration and settlement of the great uninhabited American continent. It is also something of a true-life mystery, for the gaps in the prehistory of American Indians are many. They had no means to record their story until the day when European observers could put their observations and impressions into words. Therefore, we must rely on the material evidence that was left behind and the conclusions of contemporary scholars who have given voice to their silent relics. Because academic theories are educated speculations until proven or disproven, the reader will not be surprised at such qualifying words as "maybe," "likely," and "probably."

THE EASTERN WOODLANDS

ND MN SD NE IA KS MO OK AR TX

L. SUPERIOR WI L. MICHIGAN MI L. HURON L. ONTARIO L. ERIE IL IN OH KY WV VA TN NC MS AL GA LA FL SC

ME VT NH NY MA CT RI PA NJ DE MD

0 100 200 300
MILES

The history of the Woodland Indians is especially intriguing. They were the first to suffer staggering losses to foreign diseases, for their eighteen thousand years of New World isolation gave them no immunity. And they were the first to be fragmented and dispersed by the colonial invasions that overwhelmed them.

Their tribal lands held the eastern mix of evergreens and hardwood trees, with their nut and fruit sustenance, that attracted both man and beast. If one could walk tall along the crests of the Appalachian Mountains, one would see the woodland region extending eastward to the Atlantic coastline, southward to the Gulf of Mexico, westward to the Mississippi River, and northward to the Great Lakes and the St. Lawrence River Valley. A few scattered Paleo-

1

Indian hunting bands had made their way across the country after Ice Age game and arrived in the woodlands at least 30,000 years ago. Much of what we now know of these hardy newcomers and the progress of their kin up to the time of the European Contact Period will appear in the following pages.

Looking still further back, before the Asia-to-Alaska migrations across the Bering Strait (which made the great American adventure possible), it's hard to imagine that no human had ever set foot on this unknown continent. Elsewhere in the world there was that vague and distant past when all prehuman forms followed the same long and dangerous path of survival. They lived by their wits, experimenting with chipped stone tools that made life easier and could reduce fearsome animals to a ready source of food and clothing. Only about ten thousand years after becoming full-fledged modern Homo sapiens, a few hunting bands took their one-way trip into this New World, bringing their stone-crafting traditions with them.

Without any prehistoric contact, there could be no sharing of the new technology that developed beyond the American shorelines. The isolated American Indian remained a Stone Age people while their Asian kin progressed with the rest of the world. A very brief look at the earliest beginnings of mankind will give some background for the primitive stone tools that would be one day perfected by the Native Americans in general and the Woodland Indians in particular.

OUR EARLIEST ANCESTORS

Back when those outsized reptiles, the dinosaurs, lumbered across their primitive landscape, there also were tiny, squirrel~like animals that kept out of harm's way by keeping to the treetops. Not only were they warm~blooded and endowed with a generous supply of brain cells, but they also fed their young milk from their mammary glands. They ~ and we ~ are therefore known as mammals. When the dinosaurs disappeared over sixty million years ago, these prosimians were free to begin a remark~ able series of changes in form, increased brain capacity, and ability.

Twenty million years later, in the warmth of the Asian and African jungles, their family tree had branched into the earliest forms of monkeys and apes. Within another ten million years, a quite different branch had sprouted from the prosimian stock. Preman had arrived.

THE ORIENTAL TREE SHREWS
RESEMBLE THE EARLIEST PRIMATES

Australopithecus Africanus:
3,000,000 to 2,000,000 B.P. (Before Present)

THE EARLIEST HAND AXE
WAS NOTHING MORE THAN
ROUNDISH STONE WITH A
ROUGHLY CHIPPED CUTTING
EDGE.

At first glance, this hominid (manlike) species didn't look all that different from its ape cousins. ("Pithecoid" means "apelike," "australo" is for southern, and "africanus" for the land of first discovery.) But a larger brain, filled with inquisitiveness, brought these creatures out of the treetops and onto the ground to search out a wider variety of edibles. Since its upper extremities were no longer needed for branch~ to~branch swinging, the australopithecine was able to hold a fist~sized stone to crack nuts and, if need be, the skull of a predator. A few chips, knocked off one end by trial and error, gave an edge better used for cutting than mashing. (Known as the Oldowai Tradition, the technique was named after the first discovery site, at Olduvai Gorge, Tanzania.)

Homo Erectus: 2,000,000 to 300,000 B.P.

"Erect man" stepped upright into the evolutionary picture with an enlarged frontal brain that could handle rudimentary thought. His (or her) upper and lower limbs were not unlike modern man's, and his increased dexterity allowed him to make more sophisticated tools. With the hand axe used by his predecessors, erectus was able to strike sharp flakes and slivers from a stone core. With the chips, he could at last slice through the tough hide and meat of his catch. The core itself became a hand axe, which was chipped on both sides of one end for a sharpened edge. (Known as the Acheulean Tradition, this technical innovation was named after the discovery site at St. Acheul, France, and introduced the Old Stone Age.)

Armed with this formidable weapon, erectus could take on game as large as a camel or even a mammoth. Members of his family could plan a cooperative attack. Smoldering coals, nursed along after a natural happening such as a fire started by lightning or a volcanic eruption, could be fanned to life to start a grass fire. Fleeing before the flames, the beasts stampeded over a cliff or became mired in a swamp ahead. Once helpless, they could be easily dispatched.

It was once thought that erectus was the missing link between man and monkey. Billed as the remains of *Dawn Man* or *Piltdown Man* (named after the discovery site in England), a humanoid skull with an apelike jaw discovered in 1912 made all the headlines. Only after flourine dating was discovered in the 1950s was it realized that some jokester had planted a modern skull with an orangutan jaw.

Overshadowed by the publicity surrounding the discovery of the "Piltdown Man" was "Java Man," found in the East Indies in 1891 and largely ignored. Also eclipsed was "Peking Man," discovered in 1927 in a limestone cave near that Chinese city. It seems that the locals had been digging up such fossilized bones for centuries and grinding them into medicinal potions. Rescued from becoming "Powder Man," it had the same characteristics as the Java Homo erectus — a high crown sloping down to heavy brow projections, almost no chin despite a heavy jaw, and an estimated height of about 4 feet. Only

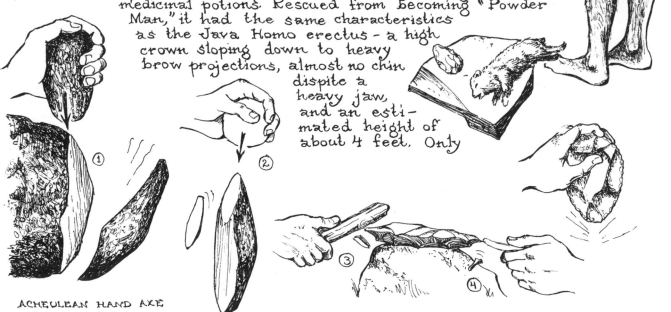

ACHEULEAN HAND AXE

A HAND-SIZED SLAB OF FLINT ① WAS FIRST STRUCK FROM A STONE CORE WITH A HAMMERSTONE. LIGHTER HAMMERSTONE BLOWS SEPARATED FLAKES FROM THE UNDERSIDES OF THE SLAB ② TO ROUGH OUT THE SHAPE AND THICKNESS OF THE HAND AXE. FINALLY, GENTLE DOWNWARD TAPS WITH A HARDWOOD STICK ③ OR PRESSURE FLAKING WITH AN ANTLER HORN ④ MADE AN EFFICIENT CUTTER.

after the English hoax was revealed did "Java Man" and "Peking Man" at last take their place as legitimate links in the human chain.

Homo Sapiens (Archaic): 300,000 to 100,000 B.P.

It was in the summer of 1992 that archaeologists discovered the next great step in human evolution. A cave in northern Spain's Sierra de Atapuerca held a surprising dissimilar group of fossilized skulls. Some had small brain cases and large protruding faces that had the unmistakable stamp of erectus evolving into pre-Neanderthals. And there were others with large brain capacities and smaller faces that more closely resembled modern man. The family tree had branched again to produce early primitive Neanderthals and our own more brainy relatives, the Cro-Magnons. Both had developed enough survival skills to weather a brutal deep freeze some two hundred thousand years ago. Perhaps it was a change in the angle of rotation of the earth's axis that denied the sun's warmth. At any rate, the bitter northern cold lasted for seventy-five thousand years as the glaciers expanded southward. The two Homo sapiens prototypes saw it through and entered the last interglacial period one hundred twenty-five thousand years ago. Happily, the climate warmed to our present day temperatures, and by 100,000 B.P. the early Neanderthals and Cro-Magnons had matured with more differences than similarities.

Homo Sapiens (Neanderthal): 125,000 to 35,000 B.P.

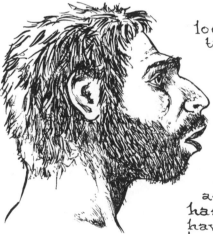

NEANDERTHAL MAN

The Neanderthal hadn't lost its apish look. The heavy bone structure was sheathed in the same powerful muscles that characterized its chunky Homo erectus ancestors. Its ski-sloped forehead still projected into heavy brow ridges that receded so far back its face was nearly chinless. When a Neanderthal fossil was first discovered in a German limestone quarry in the Neander Valley (Neander Thal in German) in 1856, Victorians suffered acute embarrassment. An ancestor that was a cross between the hunchback of Notre Dame and a squatty ape with dangling arms was hard to accept. Its limbs and trunk did indeed have different proportions than those of its horrified discoverers.

But archaeologists of that time had confused two Homo sapiens, the Neanderthal and the modern. The Neanderthals had been swinging from a different branch than modern man and women's family tree. Perhaps some genes may have been swapped between the two developing species, but there could be no mistaking the differences in the skeletal remains — or their similarities. With brains of about the same size as modern humans, they shared the title of Homo sapiens, or "wise men." They could certainly think out limited problems that couldn't be solved by brute strength. The two species probably coexisted peacefully throughout the Old World without a hint of conflict. Yet by 50,000 B.P. the Neanderthals had mysteriously disappeared — perhaps caught up in a regressing genetic pool, outmaneuvered for food and resources in the last Ice Age, or simply absorbed by modern man. They did hang on the isolation of Western Europe until 35,000 years ago, when that area was occupied exclusively by modern humans.

NEANDERTHAL AND MODERN MAN SHARED THE MOUSTERIAN TOOL KIT TECHNIQUE.

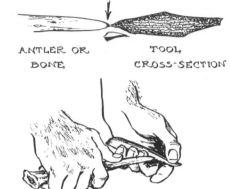

ANTLER OR BONE

TOOL CROSS-SECTION

A FLINT NODULE WAS DIVIDED TO GIVE A FLAT STRIKING SURFACE.

LONG BLADES WERE STRUCK FROM THE CORE THAT WERE 1½ TO 3 INCHES IN LENGTH.

PRESSURE FLAKING ALONG THE BLADE EDGES GAVE SHAPE AND SHARPNESS TO THE TOOL.

Homo Sapiens (Modern): 100,000 B.P. and Ongoing

As a rule of thumb, the more brain power, the less the muscle power needed for adaptability. Our ancestors were certainly adaptable as they spread out over the world, except for the unknown and uninhabited American continent. New environments and changing sperm gene pools produced a variety of races that made the humans anything but humdrum and boring.

All these scattered peoples honed their tool-making skills with a new way to strike long flakes from fine-grained stone cores. (Called the Mousterian Tradition, it is named after the discovery site at Le Moustier, France.) The flakes could be chipped into a variety of useful tools — axes, choppers, borers, knives, scrapers, planes, serrated saw blades, and chisels. Their thrusting spears and throwing lances were a far cry from the primitive hand axes of their forebears. Some shafts were simply fire-hardened into tapered points, while others were tipped with chipped stone, bone, or ivory points.

MOUSTERIAN FLINT FLAKE TOOLS

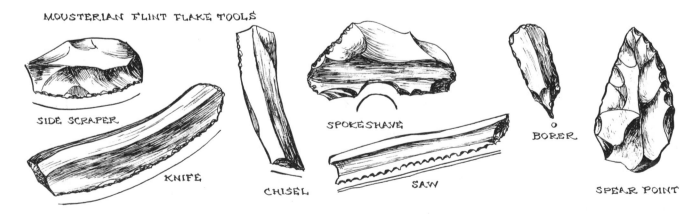

SIDE SCRAPER

KNIFE

CHISEL

SPOKESHAVE

SAW

BORER

SPEAR POINT

Experience had shown that fine-grained stones could be flaked and chipped in any direction to give conchoidal, or shell-like, fractures. Dark gray or black flint, found as boulder cores, and the lighter colored chert that was split from rockbeds were favorites. So, too, was the brown or black obsidian, a natural glass from volcanic flows. Although quartz and quartzite did have a glasslike crystalline makeup, they yielded no conchoidal fractures, as do glasslike stones. They could still be shaped into less delicate implements when the others were not on hand.

CONCHOIDAL FRACTURE

Late Magdalenian art kept pace with the creativity shown in the stone tool craftsmanship. These artistic examples date back to about 20,000 B.P.

CAVE PAINTING OF A BISON
WITH ATLATL DART WOUNDS
NIAUX CAVERN, SOUTHWESTERN FRANCE

PAINTED WALL ENGRAVING OF A HORSE
NIAUX CAVERN, SOUTHEASTERN FRANCE

ENGRAVING ON IVORY OF A MAMMOTH
LA MADELEINE, FRANCE

1 THE ANCESTORS OF THE WOODLAND INDIANS

With their well-crafted stone implements, modern man and woman were able to hunt and clothe the family. They were ready for the last great ice age, the Wisconsin, with its periodic glacial buildups that covered the more northerly reaches of the world 80,000 to 20,000 years ago. There were small groups of hunters who were actually stalking their game up and into the sub-Arctic glacial reaches. Their traces in Siberia have been dated back to at least 35,000 years ago.

Notable among those hardy souls were members of the Diuktai culture — small family hunting bands who migrated from China and Japan. Their destination was northern China's glacial country, where the tundra and broad grasslands invited Ice Age beasts to graze. The Diuktai penetrated well into Siberia by following the Pechora River Valley northward. Their temporary shelters were little more than rock overhangs with, perhaps, the added protection of hide-covered lean-tos. The refrigeration of their meat wasn't much of a problem, but how they built fires for cooking or warmth is anyone's guess.

The Diuktai found their game in the boggy Siberian valleys below the Arctic Circle. The surrounding mountains were iced more than a mile in thickness, for their heights effectively relieved the moisture-laden winds of their burden. The ice-free lowlands attracted woolly mammoths, mastodons, musk oxen, caribou (Europeans

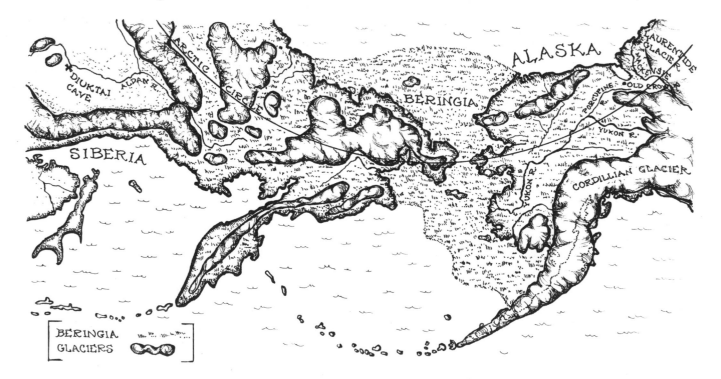

know them as reindeer), moose (Europeans call them elk), long-horned bison, and deer. A family band could isolate and dispatch the young and the weak from a herd, trap even the largest animals in camouflaged pits near watering holes, or use the old stampeding tactics of their *Homo erectus* predecessors.

Nearby, the grasslands of the Chukchi Peninsula extended down to the shores of the Bering Strait. On a clear day, a hunter could make out a land of some sort a short 56 miles away. Today it's known as Alaska. There were times during the great glacial buildups when both man and beast could walk the distance with dry feet and hoofs. Sea winds carried moisture to the frigid mountaintops, where the icy blanket could grow to a thickness of 2 miles. The sea water evaporated, lowering the oceans worldwide, and the flat and shallow bottom of the Bering Strait soon became exposed ~ so much so that it became a huge 1,000-mile-wide connection between Asia and the unknown American continent. We know the joined lowlands of Siberia and Alaska as Beringia.

The Diuktai hunters were likely more intent on tracking their quarry than taking notice of the grassy stretch that had surfaced in the ocean. Once they crossed over onto Alaskan soil, they took their place in the history of a great unknown and uninhabited continent. They would thereafter be known as the Paleo Indians, the ancient relatives of most of America's Indian people. But just when did they first arrive? Archaeologists have knocked heads over the question for decades. Fortunately, we now have new discoveries, carefully made excavations, and sophisticated dating methods with some surprising answers.

We know that the last ice age, the Wisconsin, experienced the most extensive glacial advances 45,000, 28,000, and 22,000 years ago. The Bering Strait land bridge was dry and walkable for thousands of years before and after these great icy buildups. The periodic thaws would then drown the passage and again separate Asia from America. Most investigators feel the evidence points to a first crossing of at least 30,000 years ago, although there is still an occasional holdout for a more recent 15,000 years. It may be that both dates are correct and that a series of crossings were made each time a periodic deep freeze connected the two continents. There is even a possibility that the first crossing took place at a very early 55,000 years ago. But until we

TIME SPANS WHEN THE BERING STRAIT BRIDGE WAS PASSABLE
— AS SHOWN IN CHECKERED AREAS —

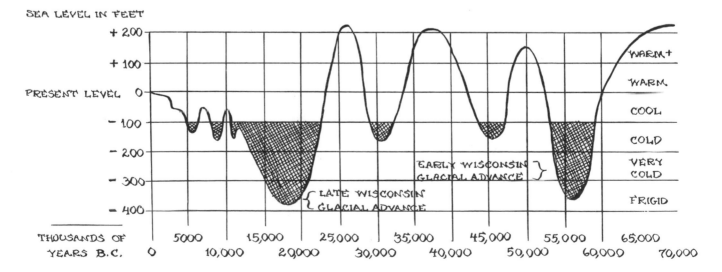

uncover more weighty evidence, the 30,000-year date remains our best guesstimate.

THE PALEO-AMERICAN INDIANS
30,000 to 8000 B.C.

The few wandering bands of Diuktai hunters might not have realized that their ongoing search for game led them anywhere but their Asian homeland. Their concern was survival, and they brought with them refined skills of flint knapping. Their spear points, brought over from Asia, are known by archaeologists as the Sandia Type I, a thick point with a projecting shoulder that may have served as a barb. Its rounded base was hafted into a bone foreshaft socket; both remained in the quarry until it dropped from its wounds. Meanwhile, the spear shaft could be retrieved and rearmed while the hunter tracked the injured beast.

Perhaps the greatest breakthrough for a people so dependent on meat and hide clothing was the spear-throwing stick. Specimens have been found that date from before 20,000 B.C. Most were crafted of antler, with a hole bored at the junction of the main stem and the brow-tine joint. They were once thought to be wrenches to straighten out still-pliable bone foreshafts that would be socketed into the spear shaft. Perhaps so. But as a spear-throwing device, a hunter could add a foot or so to his throwing arm, increasing the arc of throw considerably. More distant targets could be hit with a greater force. (By 5,000 B.C. the rigid stick would be replaced by a weighted, flexible atlatl for more power and distance.)

THE ENGRAVINGS ON THIS RIGID SPEAR THROWER INCLUDE A HUNTER AT THE READY WITH HIS OWN WEAPON. ITS DISCOVERY SITE WAS LA MADELEINE, FRANCE.

The newcomers inched their way inland along Alaska's Yukon River valleys, with their profusion of grass and tundra. Formidable ice-sheathed mountains loomed on either side, preventing them from traveling in any direction other than an eastward course. Beyond the Yukon, they followed along the Porcupine River and then on to the Crow River Valley. In this most distant reach of Beringia, a number of important artifacts have been found and dated about 13,000 B.C. Yet there was a caribou-bone flesher (used for skinning hides) that could date to 25,000 B.C. At Old Crow, there was evidence that domesticated wolves, used as hunting dogs, accompanied the earliest crossings. The jaws of several had a possible radiocarbon date of 28,000 B.C., which is most unusual, since artifact discoveries are generally surface finds because of the impenetrable permafrost or rocky elevations used as hunting lookouts. Without the stratigraphic layering necessary for uncontaminated carbon dating, surface finds must remain forever mute.

We assume each hunting band was an extended family unit~perhaps no more than twenty-five to fifty members in all. Their very existance depended on the protection and hunting skills of the menfolk,

THE COMPOUND SPEAR AND ITS BATON SPEAR~THROWER

THE TIME~HONORED THRUSTING AND THROWING SPEAR WAS IMPROVED BY SNUGGING A FORE~
SHAFT INTO A MAINSHAFT SOCKET. THE FORESHAFT OF THE COMPOUND SPEAR WOULD REMAIN
EMBEDDED IN THE WOUNDED GAME WHILE THE WOODEN MAINSHAFT WAS RETRIEVED AND
ARMED WITH ANOTHER FORESHAFT FOR A LATER KILL.

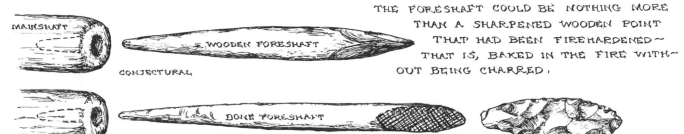

THE FORESHAFT COULD BE NOTHING MORE
THAN A SHARPENED WOODEN POINT
THAT HAD BEEN FIREHARDENED~
THAT IS, BAKED IN THE FIRE WITH~
OUT BEING CHARRED.

MAINSHAFT

WOODEN FORESHAFT
CONJECTURAL

BONE FORESHAFT

A SHOULDERED FLINT POINT, THE SANDIA I ~ FIRST DISCOVERED AT THE SANDIA CAVE, NEW MEXICO~
WAS BROUGHT FROM THE ASIAN HOMELANDS. THE SHOULDER ACTED AS A BARB WHEN LASHED TO
THE BONE FORESHAFT. IT MAY HAVE BEEN IN USE FOR 60,000 YEARS OR MORE. *

THE BONE HARPOON
WITH DECORATED
BARBS WAS ITS OWN FORESHAFT.
THE KNOBS ON THE STEM HELD A TIED
LINE, HANDY FOR RETRIEVAL. BETWEEN
16,000 AND 9,000 B.C., REMARKABLE
CRAFTSMANSHIP IN BONE PRODUCED
THIS AND OTHER ARTISTRY ~ SUCH AS
THE SPEARTHROWER HORSE
SHOWN HERE.

BATON
SPEAR~THROWERS

BY EXTENDING THE HUNTER'S THROWING
ARM WITH A SPEAR~THROWER, SPEED, RANGE,
AND FORCE OF IMPACT WERE GREATLY INCREASED.
THESE EARLY SPEAR~THROWERS WERE FASHIONED
FROM WOOD FOR THE MOST PART. ONLY THOSE OF BONE
AND ANTLER SURVIVED THE MILLENNIA. WHEN FIRST
DISCOVERED A CENTURY AGO, THEY WERE THOUGHT TO BE
STATUS SYMBOLS AND ARE STILL KNOWN AS "BATON DE
COMMANDEMENTS."
THE BATON SPEAR~THROWER WAS AN EARLY
VERSION OF THE MORE EFFICIENT ATLATL
SPEAR~THROWER. ALTHOUGH THE LAUNCHING
METHOD IS UNKNOWN, THERE
ARE WORKABLE THEORIES THAT
INCLUDE A LASHED LEATHER THONG. *
AFTER PASSING IT THROUGH THE
LAUNCHER HOLE AND
SPIRALED AROUND

THE SPEAR FOR A
STRAIGHTER FLIGHT, THE
KNOTTED END IS LOOPED
AND CAUGHT. THE THUMB
AND FOREFINGER OF THE
THROWING HAND HOLD THE SPEAR THONG UNDER TENSION
WHILE THE LAST THREE FINGERS HOLD THE SPEAR~THROWER. THE
SPEAR IS WHIPPED FORWARD WITH AN OVERHAND PITCH.

* BULLETIN OF PRIMITIVE TECHNOLOGY, VOL. 1, NO. 4

providing a patrilineal base for their family life. The female would join her chosen male's band and the children would become members at birth. While the men were off on their cooperative hunting ventures, the women and children remained within the protection of the base camp foraging for whatever roots, greens, and fruits they could find to supplement their diet of meat or perhaps fish. The danger of hungry predators was real, for saber-tooth tigers, bears, giant wolves, and jaguars weren't fussy about who or what they had for lunch.

DOMESTICATED WOLF

The features of the newcomers hinted of their early Asian ancestry. The women probably had some degree of the Mongolian skin fold over their eyes. Both sexes had scooped, shovel-shaped teeth, sturdy builds, light skin that tanned easily, and straight black hair without graying or baldness. The Asian latecomers of some five to six thousand years ago~ Eskimo, Apache, Navajo, Pima, and Yuman peoples~ had the more typical Oriental characteristics.

When the few Paleo bands entered into their American isolation, their gene pool remained unchanged by outside races. For the most part, present-day American Indians still carry the O-type blood group of the ancient ancestors. Later arrivals brought Group B to Alaska, while Group A is confined to Canada. Many who claim an Indian heritage today are so diluted with these tell-tale blood markers that their ancestry is very much in doubt. Recent research involving the DNA arrangements within the mitochondria of the body's cells may help to sort out the Paleo~American Indians' direct descendants. These mitochondrial genes are separate from the body's genes and are passed on to children only by the mother, not the father. By comparing the blood samples from the various Indian tribes, the possibility has been raised that most American Indians are descended from just four women who made the Bering crossing. Time will tell.

When the Paleo hunters left the rest of the world behind, they also freed themselves from the contagious diseases that plagued their Asian relatives. Without carrier contact, there could be no smallpox, measles, typhoid, or typhus. While this was a blessing, there could be no acquired immunity through repeated exposures. Many centuries in the future, when European explorers, traders, and settlers came to America, whole villages would be wiped out by simple childhood diseases or even the common cold.

Once the hunting bands reached the Mackenzie River, they were at a dead end. Boxed in by mountainous glaciers ahead and with no retreat to Asia, they stumbled upon an escape route. The Ice Age animals had long followed the Mackenzie River Valley to their northern grazing grounds. When warming trends melted the world's glacial masses, raising the ocean's level and again flooding the Bering Strait, the Mackenzie corridor opened as well. Actually, it was more an obstacle course than a passageway. The melting ice made a wide and roaring river that dashed over glacial rocks between two receding ice walls. Mosses, lichen, and sedge took hold, probably encouraging game to migrate both north and south. When the few hunting bands won their way down the wet and rocky highway between the Laurentide and the Cordilleran glaciers, they must have been heartened by the willow, birch, spruce, and fir that made their timid debuts along the way.

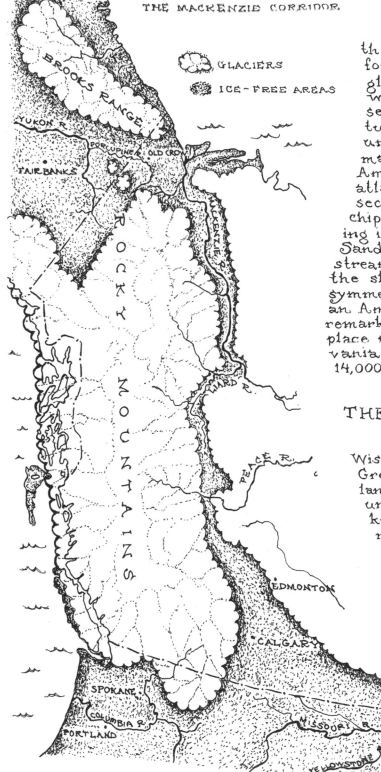

THE MACKENZIE CORRIDOR

☁ GLACIERS

░ ICE-FREE AREAS

BROOKS RANGE

YUKON R.

PORCUPINE • OLD CROW

FAIRBANKS

ROCKY MOUNTAINS

MACKENZIE R.

LIARD R.

PEACE R.

EDMONTON

CALGARY

SPOKANE

COLUMBIA R.

PORTLAND

MISSOURI R.

YELLOWSTONE R.

Near the present border of the United States and Canada, the foot of the great Laurentide glacier opened and veered eastward. Rivers, bogs, and mires seemed to lace the expanses of tundra. There, a variety of game, unfamiliar with human predators, made easy targets. The Paleo-Americans found that the bulky atlatl spear point could be more securely hafted by striking off chips from the basal faces, resulting in what is now referred to as the Sandia Type II point. Then they streamlined the point by chipping away the shoulder, creating the thinned and symmetrical pre-Clovis point that was an American innovation. It is most remarkable that its discovery took place near far-off Pittsburgh, Pennsylvania — and with the early date of 14,000 B.C.

THE NORTHEASTERN TRAIL

At the height of the last great Wisconsin glacial advance, the Great Lakes region, all of New England, and all of Long Island were under a mile-thick ice blanket. We know that the Paleo hunters reached Pennsylvania around that time because, about 40 miles southwest of Pittsburgh, University of Pittsburgh archaeologists unearthed that Sandia Type II point in the Meadowcroft Rock Shelter. One or more bands had stalked the tundra along the glacial base and eastward after the retreating game. They stopped at Meadowcroft shelter because its hillside overlooked a swampy valley with lush grasses. It was an ideal game lookout for the hunters, and in the northeast, that game would have been predominantly

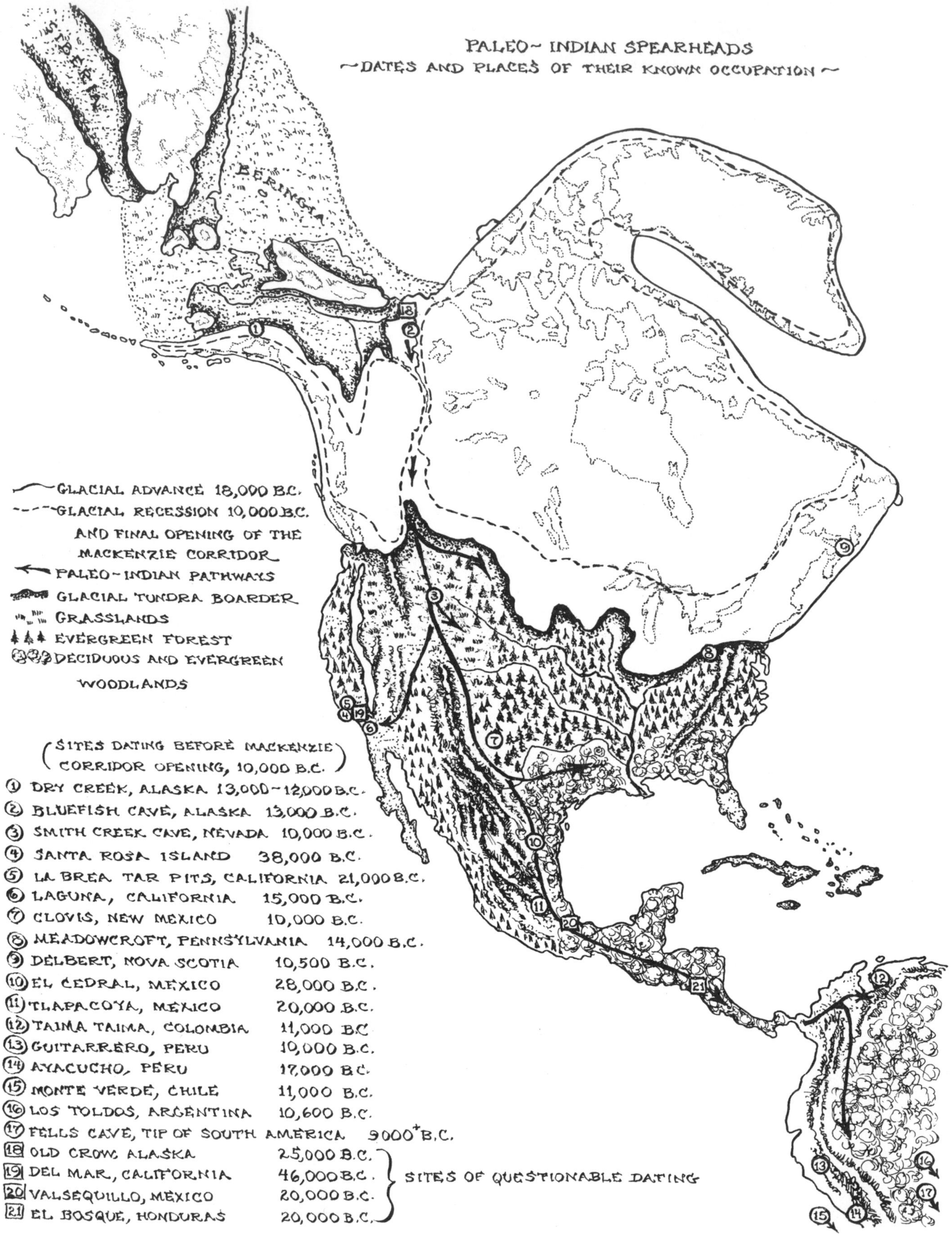

PALEO~INDIAN SPEARHEADS
~DATES AND PLACES OF THEIR KNOWN OCCUPATION~

SIBERIA

BERINGIA

GLACIAL ADVANCE 18,000 B.C.
GLACIAL RECESSION 10,000 B.C.
AND FINAL OPENING OF THE
MACKENZIE CORRIDOR
PALEO~INDIAN PATHWAYS
GLACIAL TUNDRA BOARDER
GRASSLANDS
EVERGREEN FOREST
DECIDUOUS AND EVERGREEN
WOODLANDS

(SITES DATING BEFORE MACKENZIE)
CORRIDOR OPENING, 10,000 B.C.

① DRY CREEK, ALASKA 13,000~12,000 B.C.
② BLUEFISH CAVE, ALASKA 13,000 B.C.
③ SMITH CREEK CAVE, NEVADA 10,000 B.C.
④ SANTA ROSA ISLAND 38,000 B.C.
⑤ LA BREA TAR PITS, CALIFORNIA 21,000 B.C.
⑥ LAGUNA, CALIFORNIA 15,000 B.C.
⑦ CLOVIS, NEW MEXICO 10,000 B.C.
⑧ MEADOWCROFT, PENNSYLVANIA 14,000 B.C.
⑨ DELBERT, NOVA SCOTIA 10,500 B.C.
⑩ EL CEDRAL, MEXICO 28,000 B.C.
⑪ TLAPACOYA, MEXICO 20,000 B.C.
⑫ TAIMA TAIMA, COLOMBIA 11,000 B.C.
⑬ GUITARRERO, PERU 10,000 B.C.
⑭ AYACUCHO, PERU 17,000 B.C.
⑮ MONTE VERDE, CHILE 11,000 B.C.
⑯ LOS TOLDOS, ARGENTINA 10,600 B.C.
⑰ FELLS CAVE, TIP OF SOUTH AMERICA 9000+ B.C.
⑱ OLD CROW, ALASKA 25,000 B.C.
⑲ DEL MAR, CALIFORNIA 46,000 B.C.
⑳ VALSEQUILLO, MEXICO 20,000 B.C.
㉑ EL BOSQUE, HONDURAS 20,000 B.C.

SITES OF QUESTIONABLE DATING

14

caribou. The pre-Clovis point that saw duty there was the forerunner to that all-round Paleo favorite, the fluted Clovis point.

PROGRESS IN SPEAR LAUNCHING

FEMALE

COMBINATION

MALE

THE ATLATL DART-THROWER CAME INTO USE BY 10,000 B.C.. LIKE THE BATON SPEAR-THROWER, ITS SHAFT COULD BE LAUNCHED WITH CONSIDERABLE POWER FOR GREAT DISTANCES. THE REASON WAS CENTRIFUGAL FORCE. (MUCH LATER, GOLIATH WAS LEVELED BY THE SAME PRINCIPLE WHEN DAVID WHIRLED A SLING-HELD STONE.) WITH THE PALEO-INDIAN HUNTER'S ARM SO LENGTHENED, HE COULD STRIKE A TARGET SOME 300 FEET AWAY. FOR A HAND-HELD SHAFT, 50 TO 75 FEET WOULD BE TOPS. THE DART COULD BE LAUNCHED FROM AN ATLATL PROJECTION OR A GROOVE.

FORESHAFT

SANDIA I WITH BASAL CHIP

PRE-CLOVIS SHOULDER REMOVED

THE COMPOUND SPEAR HAD BEEN SHORTENED TO BETWEEN 4 AND 5 FEET TO BECOME THE ATLATL DART, FLETCHED WITH THREE FEATHERS FOR A STRAIGHTER FLIGHT. NOT UNTIL A.D. 700 TO 900 WAS THIS IMPORTANT WEAPON REPLACED BY THE BOW AND ARROW.

Symmetrical faces with a single, long flake groove extending halfway up from the concave base~ these were the hallmarks of the Clovis spear point. They would spell success and survival for the remainder of the Paleo-Indian period from before 10,000 to 8000 B.C. The largest concentration of bands was in the East, particularly Ohio, Kentucky, Virginia, and Massachusetts. Their discovery sites help map the northeastern wanderings of these nomadic bands. River valleys, gouged out by the receding glaciers, offered easier travel for the hunters.

The great glacial thaw had been underway since 15,000 B.C. Warmer temperatures had encouraged stands of red and jack pine, spruce, and birch where grass, sedge, and lichen once grew. It was a mixed blessing, for the Ice Age beasts were following the retreating glaciers northward. Animals such as the mastodon (from the Latin "breast-tooth") had ripple-shaped

THE CLOVIS POINT

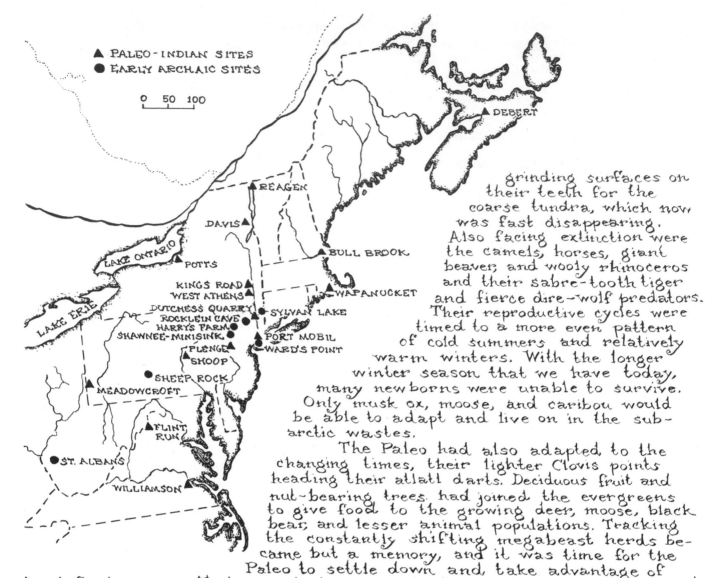

grinding surfaces on their teeth for the coarse tundra, which now was fast disappearing. Also facing extinction were the camels, horses, giant beaver, and wooly rhinoceros and their sabre-tooth tiger and fierce dire-wolf predators. Their reproductive cycles were timed to a more even pattern of cold summers and relatively warm winters. With the longer winter season that we have today, many newborns were unable to survive. Only musk ox, moose, and caribou would be able to adapt and live on in the sub-arctic wastes.

The Paleo had also adapted to the changing times, their lighter Clovis points heading their atlatl darts. Deciduous fruit and nut-bearing trees had joined the evergreens to give food to the growing deer, moose, black bear, and lesser animal populations. Tracking the constantly shifting megabeast herds became but a memory, and it was time for the Paleo to settle down and take advantage of local food sources. Turkey and other game birds were becoming plentiful, and there were roots, nuts, fruits, and greens nearby for foraging. There is even evidence that the people along the Delaware River added fish to their diet.

The growing number of family bands laid claim to their hunting lands. These were usually in river valleys, where the Paleo used the evergreen hills and mountains as territorial boundaries. The campsites varied. Some were lone hilltop lookouts, such as the Meadowcroft rock shelter or the Shoop site near Harrisburg. At these sites, usually only hunting artifacts were found. The hunters' kin would remain behind in the small family shelters. There, one would expect to find a collection of knives, scrapers, gravers, awls, spokeshaves, and the flint cores that supplied these tools. The Shawnee-Minisink site by the Delaware River and the Templeton site in Washington, Connecticut, are good examples.

FLAKE KNIFE   END-SCRAPER   SIDE-SCRAPER   BORER   SPOKESHAVE   GRAVER   DRILL

16

There were also large-band camps that served as seasonal gathering places for family groups. It was the social event of the year for between fifty and two hundred people of all ages and both sexes— a time for giving gifts of finely crafted tools and Clovis points of colorful cherts from distant quarries. It was also a time for romance. New mates would live with the male's band, where he could continue his hunting partnerships and protect his squatter's rights where his extended family had settled. Intermating encouraged friendly relationships between the small segmented groups that one day might join in a common village life. Such camp examples would include the Plenge site in New Jersey, Bull Brook in Massachusetts, and the Debert site in distant Nova Scotia.

Finally, large band hunting camps brought different bands together for a cooperative hunt. Camp life was a bustle of activity, for women and children were there as well. A wide range of tools and weapons were crafted and used at the camps, including knives, drills, spokeshaves, and flint flakes for butchering and wood and leather work. Port Mobil, on western Staten Island, would be such a site.

SPINNING A WOODEN DRILL
GAVE FIRE BY FRICTION.

There are times when archaeologists can learn from what **wasn't** present at a dig. For example, no iron pyrites have been found at a Paleo site. We must assume, then, that iron pyrites and flint were not used for strike-a-light fire building. At the Paleo-period Guitarreo Cave in the Andes Mountains, however, wooden fire drills for friction fires were used— and perhaps by more northerly kin as well. Because no mortars and pestles for pulverizing nuts and roots have been unearthed, we also know that their foraged additions to the heavy meat diet went unground. Furthermore, no heavy woodworking tools have been discovered, and therefore no dugout canoes were in service. The Paleo may have crossed rivers by using portable boats with hide-covered saplings lashed in a half-sphere shape or by following the rivers until a ford or iced-over stretch of water could be found.

Our notions of Paleo-Indian clothing are also speculative. But considering the fine bone needles discovered and plentiful animal pelts, their garments must have been fitted and snug for any wintry chill. Creating such wear was women's work, for only at the band camps are needles, knives, and borers found, never at the men's hunting camps. The acidic soil of the East was a poor preserver of such organic material, unlike Oregon's Fort Rock Cave, where the oldest known footwear was found.

The Paleo-Indians' wandering ways and big-game hunting were all but forgotten by 8000 B.C., though the time-honored Clovis-pointed dart and atlatl were still bringing down smaller wildlife. Some larger targets, such as the woodland bison, caribou, and moose, still remained, but changing forests and expert marksmanship cut deeply into their numbers. Meanwhile the white-tailed deer and bear had taken kindly to the deciduous nut-bearing woodlands and replaced most of the Ice Age game. Lesser critters—

BULL-BOAT
AMERICAN PLAINS INDIANS

17

beaver, raccoon, fox, muskrat, skunk, squirrel, turkey, and waterfowl ~ were also taken. With quarry so small and wary, the atlatl dart must have been a deadly weapon.

THE SOUTHEASTERN PALEO-AMERICAN PATHWAY

Some of several bands who had made safe passage through the Mackenzie Corridor drifted southward instead of along the glacial bounds. Beyond the tundra, the western prairies opened into a rich savannah of seemingly endless grasslands that were dotted with clusters of trees. There grazed the wooly mammoth herds, horses, camels, and long-horned bison. The hunters found the easiest way to take this bonanza of game was to stampede the herds with grass fires or form a noisy, moving arc of hunters. In the confusion that followed, great numbers could be driven over a cliff or into one of many melt-off mires. The badly injured beasts or those hopelessly trapped in the muck could be dispatched without danger. It was certainly overkill, for only a tiny fraction of the meat could be used before it all spoiled. The horse became extinct on the North American continent without the Early Americans ever realizing its potential for work and transportation. That must await its re-introduction during the six~ teenth~century Spanish conquests.

The hunting bands continued to press southward, and by 9200 B.C. were camping by a freshwater pond at Clovis, New Mexico. The fluted Clovis point was first found there and so came by its name. Some hunters veered off to occupy the lower California coastline, while others continued the long journey into Mexico, on through Central America, and down to the very tip of South America. There, at Tierra del Fuego, Clovis points have been discovered that date to 9000 B.C. They represent the end of a 10,000~mile trek that began in Alaska.

Yet another Paleo-American hunting band branched off to the east. Its members were the ancestors of the southeastern woodland tribes that will be considered later in detail. The change of direction was logical, for a broad belt of deciduous forest extended from central Texas to the Atlantic coast. Nut-bearing hardwoods dominated sprinklings of spruce and pine, attracting a wide range of smaller game ~

18

deer, bear, fox, beaver, otter, raccoon, and opossum. This forest understory provided berries, shoots, and leaves for browse.

To the north, sandwiched between this warm and thriving southern country and the glacial borderlands, was a great, deep band of evergreen forests with neither grassland and tundra nor fruit-and nut-bearing trees, this food-poor region was generally shunned by wildlife. The hunting bands did likewise, venturing up some of its riverways only if game could be found there.

Late in the Paleo period, between 8500 and 7000 B.C., the hunters around the Cumberland River drainages developed an innovative atlatl dart point. Unlike the larger and heavier Clovis points that were still in use farther north, the new Cumberland points had full-length fluting and a narrowed, concave base with extended ears. Perhaps these barbs were meant to remain embedded in the animal until it dropped from its wounds. The Cumberland point did impress some Clovis holdouts, for it has been occasionally found as far north as New Jersey and the Hudson River Valley. Otherwise, the general tool kit was much the same in the Northeast and Southwest.

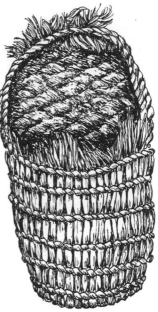

FORT ROCK CAVE IN SOUTH-CENTRAL OREGON YIELDED ALMOST 100 PAIRS OF THESE PRE-7000 B.C. SHREDDED SAGEBRUSH SANDALS.

THE EARLY ARCHAIC PERIOD:
8000 to 6000 B.C.

Now that the Paleo-Indian hunting bands were trading their nomadic lifestyle for a more settled Early Archaic existence, there was time for experimentation in their new surroundings. The climate had become warmer and drier than it is today. The cooler woodlands of the mid-Atlantic region became nearly as warm as the Southern climate, and the deciduous trees were elbowing their way into the central band of evergreen forests. The abundance of new hardwood encouraged the Early Americans to develop heavy-duty woodworking tools. It was a modest first when stone knappers roughly chipped an axe or celt to shape, then pecked a smoother surface with a pointed stone. Finally, the tool was ground and polished to give a smooth surface. Not earth-shaking, perhaps, but the advance signaled the end of the Old Stone Age in the New World and the beginning of the Neolithic or New Stone Age. Other wood-shaping tools, such as a new kind of drill and a spoke-shave scraper, joined the knives and end scrapers inherited from the Paleos at such sites as Pennsylvania's Sheep Rock Shelter and on Staten Island.

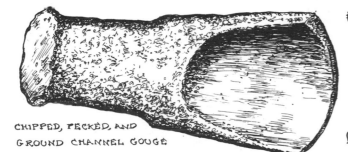

CHIPPED, PECKED, AND GROUND CHANNEL GOUGE

Their Early Archaic relatives in the New England latitudes weren't as fortunate. The evergreen forests were steadily moving northward, replacing the tundra and grasslands of the retreating glaciers. Caribou followed their grazing grounds toward the sub-arctic reaches, leaving the Early Archaics of New England with fewer game. Since nut-bearing trees had not yet arrived, the bands of the Early Archaics in this region remained small and scattered.

Although the fine art of fluting would not be seen again, the Early Archaics modified the Clovis and Cumberland designs to better target the smaller game. West of Tennessee, Kentucky, and Ohio, the corners of the point bases were generally removed for more secure lashing~ the Dalton and Plano types. Around the Mississippi River drainages and spreading eastward, the concave base of the Clovis was indented further so that it bifurcated into two barbs. The new design was called the Hardaway point. With side notching, these projections became formidable prongs that remained embedded in the game. By 7000 B.C., the bifurcation that had become diagnostic for the Early Archaic period had spread to West Virginia, then throughout the Southeast and north to New York and New England as the Kanawha point. About that same time, the flint knappers in the Carolinas were removing the corners of the bases~ quite the opposite of the bifurcated technique~ to produce the Kirk point.

For all the Early Archaics in the mixed woodlands east of the Mississippi River, seasonal hunting and gathering had become an ongoing way of life. Chance meetings of related bands at large bodies of water, such as estuaries and lakes, for shellfish and fishing renewed friendships and allowed the tribes to show off their new implements and techniques. Throughout most of the woodlands, a proto-Algonquian~ Muskhogean language was spoken during this period.

Meanwhile, the world outside America had also advanced during the Early Archaic period. For example, pottery was first made in Japan, the goat was domesticated in Persia (Iran), the first crops of wheat and barley were cultivated in the Near East, the loom was invented in the Near

CLASSIC PLUMMET

END PICK

ULU

ABRADER

THE CLOVIS POINT AND ITS EARLY ARCHAIC OFFSPRING
~THE DARKER OUTLINES SHOW EACH INNOVATION~

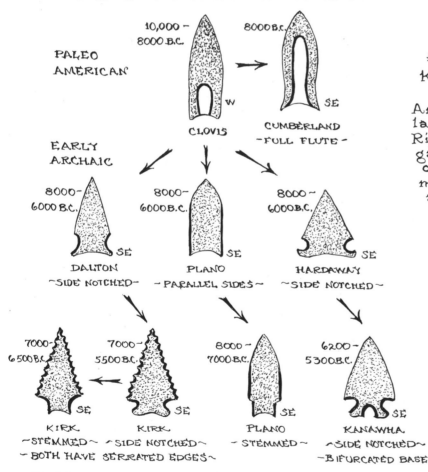

PALEO AMERICAN

10,000 - 8000 B.C.

8000 B.C.

CLOVIS W

CUMBERLAND ~FULL FLUTE~ SE

EARLY ARCHAIC

8000 - 6000 B.C.
DALTON ~SIDE NOTCHED~ SE

8000 - 6000 B.C.
PLANO ~PARALLEL SIDES~ SE

8000 - 6000 B.C.
HARDAWAY ~SIDE NOTCHED~ SE

7000 - 6500 B.C.
KIRK ~STEMMED~ SE

7000 - 5500 B.C.
KIRK ~SIDE NOTCHED~ SE

~BOTH HAVE SERRATED EDGES~

8000 - 7000 B.C.
PLANO ~STEMMED~ SE

6200 - 5300 B.C.
KANAWHA ~SIDE NOTCHED~ ~BIFURCATED BASE~ SE

IN GENERAL, SMALL POINTS WERE USED ON ATLATL DARTS AND LARGER POINTS FOR THRUSTING~THROWING SPEARS OR HAFTED AS KNIVES.

W = THROUGHOUT WOODLANDS   SE = SOUTHEAST   NE = NORTHEAST

East, and agriculture had all but replaced hunting in Europe. Such innovations that were shared all over the Old World couldn't penetrate the New World's isolation. The Early Americans were on their own.

THE MIDDLE ARCHAIC PERIOD
6000 to 4000 B.C.

The big news of the period must have been the new improvements in the atlatl. The rigid throwing stick had worked well enough against the Ice Age targets that were as big as an outsized barn door, but the fleet and wary bear, moose, white-tail deer, fox, beaver, raccoons, and game birds were another story. Some unsung Middle Archaic hunter discovered that a flexible atlatl could add considerable distance and force. It worked on the principle of today's springy fishing rod or golf club, giving a more powerful snap to the throw. This advantage was considerably increased when a weight was added to give more heft to the stick. A center hole of less than half an inch in diameter was drilled through a stone. The supple atlatl stick was then inserted in the stone and lashed to it. A rigid atlatl of that small a diameter would surely snap. These early weights were pecked and ground in the shape of wings ~ perhaps resembling a magical bird that would send the dart or spear to its target.

The corner ~ removed Kirk and the bifurcated, side-notched Kanawha points were small and lashed nicely on a dart or spear. They became the points of choice throughout most of the woodland ~ with an occasional alteration to better fit local preferences. In South Carolina and the Savannah River drainage, the Kirk was altered and is known as the Stanley Stemmed. The points used in the Southeast are called the Morrow Mountain I, and those found throughout much of the Northeast, Canada, and Labrador are known as the Stark point. If all this sounds like scrambled eggs, it must be remembered that the very survival of these Early Americans depended on the most efficient point

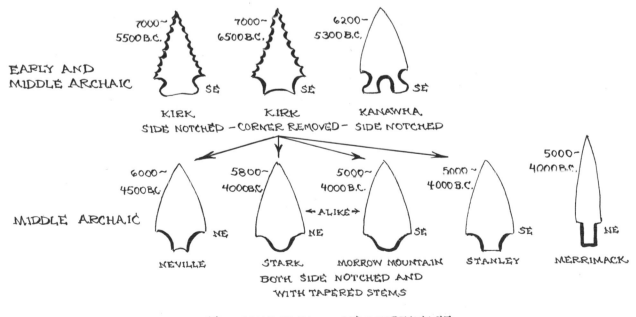

EARLY AND MIDDLE ARCHAIC

7000~5500 B.C. — KIRK SIDE NOTCHED — SE

7000~6500 B.C. — KIRK — CORNER REMOVED — SE

6200~5300 B.C. — KANAWHA SIDE NOTCHED — SE

MIDDLE ARCHAIC

6000~4500 B.C. — NEVILLE — NE

5800~4000 B.C. — STARK — NE
BOTH SIDE NOTCHED AND WITH TAPERED STEMS

←ALIKE→

5000~4000 B.C. — MORROW MOUNTAIN — SE

5000~4000 B.C. — STANLEY — SE

5000~4000 B.C. — MERRIMACK — NE

SE = SOUTHEAST   NE = NORTHEAST

ATLATL WEIGHTS

ATLATL WEIGHTS, ONCE CALLED BANNERSTONES, GAVE THE FLEXIBLE ATLATL AN EXTRA SPRING OF ENERGY BY FORCING THE WOOD FIBERS BACKWARD AS THE THROW BEGAN AND THEN FORCEFULLY REBOUNDING THEM TO HURL THE DART AT THE TARGET. THE MIDDLE ARCHAICS OF NORTH CAROLINA MAY HAVE BEEN THE ORIGINATORS OF ATLATL WEIGHTS. SOME OF THEIR SPECIMENS DATE BACK TO 6200 B.C. THE REST OF THE COUNTRY GRADUALLY FOLLOWED WITH TWO BASIC FORMS, THE UNPERFORATED AND THE PERFORATED WEIGHTS. FROM THE PACIFIC OCEAN TO THE ROCKY MOUNTAINS, THE NATIVES FAVORED THE UNPERFORATED DESIGN LASHED TO THE TOP OF THE ATLATL SHAFT.

-UNPERFORATED-

EASTWARD TO THE MISSISSIPPI RIVER, BOTH UNPERFORATED AND PERFORATED TYPES WERE USED. BUT IN THE EASTERN WOODLANDS THE PERFORATED WEIGHTS WERE PREFERRED.

PERFORATED WEIGHTS WERE OF TWO SHAPES, THE OVAL AND THE WING. BOTH HAD A FUNNEL-SHAPED HOLE THAT WEDGED ONTO THE TAPERED ATLATL SHAFT. PERHAPS SINEW WAS LASHED AROUND THE SHAFT AND ACROSS THE WEIGHT TO PREVENT THE CENTRIFUGAL FORCE OF THE THROW FROM SENDING IT FLYING.

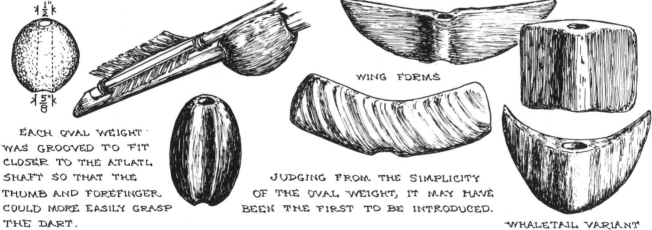

$1\frac{1}{2}$"

$\frac{5}{8}$"

EACH OVAL WEIGHT WAS GROOVED TO FIT CLOSER TO THE ATLATL SHAFT SO THAT THE THUMB AND FOREFINGER COULD MORE EASILY GRASP THE DART.

WING FORMS

JUDGING FROM THE SIMPLICITY OF THE OVAL WEIGHT, IT MAY HAVE BEEN THE FIRST TO BE INTRODUCED.

WHALETAIL VARIANT

and delivery that could be found. It is understandable that dart and spear points have been the surest means of identification before the coming of pottery styles.

At long last, the nut-bearing trees ~ perhaps hickory, walnut, chestnut, butternut, and oak ~ came to the more northern woodlands. The wildlife followed, and the few scattered bands there prospered and multiplied. In New England, the rejuvenated hunting bands adapted the Kirk corner-removed point to their own needs, creating the Neville point. Communication among the coastal bands of hunters must have been commonplace. When the later Leaf point (which looked like its namesake) was conceived down in North Carolina, the lower Merrimack River people slimmed it down and removed the corners to create the squared-stemmed Merrimack. It was a local idea that would catch fire and spread throughout the Late Archaic woodlands.

LEAF   MERRIMACK

The new dart and spear points and the weighted and flexible atlatl throwing stick were accompanied by a hunting ally, the dog. In a large shell mound along a branch of the Tennessee River ~ the Eva site ~ were found special grave pits for these domesticated hunting dogs. Dating to 5000 B.C. ~ the earliest discovery date in the woodlands ~ the skeletons seemed to be more like large Eskimo huskies than their wolflike relatives that had crossed the Bering bridge.

Hunting remained the Middle Archaic main-stay, but the gathering of nuts, seeds, and roots for flavoring, roasting, and preservation gave a welcome diet change. Evidence that this activity was pursued by the women and children (they foraged while the men hunted) is seen in the earliest pitted stone anvils for opening nuts, crude mortars, and hammerstones to be unearthed.

GROOVED PEBBLE HAMMERSTONE WITH A POSSIBLE HAFTING

NUTSTONE

MORTAR

Fishing and shellfishing had become an important part of each band's seasonal rounds. Spring fishing camps sprouted all along the coastal spawning fish runs. The discovery of many coastal harpoons indicates that there was widespread hunting for sea mammals. Along all of the woodland waterways the many plummet finds show the extent of hook-and-line and net fishing. Bone hooks and lines contributed to the catch. Shellfish were not limited to the shoreline and estuaries. Throughout the Southeast, and particularly along the branches of the Tennessee and Ohio Rivers are sizable mussel shell middens. Judging from the numbers of excavated woodworking tools, such as celts, gouges, and full-grooved ground axes, dugout canoes may have played an important part in the catching of fish and sea mammals.

23

There are indications that the Early Americans' more settled lifestyle was enriching. Some bands were joining others related by intermarriage, thereby giving added protection to their combined hunting and fishing lands. The wisest of the bands gathered in council to solve their concerns. There was time for sprucing themselves up with ornaments of drilled animal teeth, plain stone pendants, and beads of bird bone. There would seem to be concern for life after death. In the same shell mounds near the Tennessee River that held the dog burials of 5000 B.C. were flexed-position human graves.

There was a good deal of progress in the Old World as well. Cattle had been domesticated as the Middle Archaic Period opened. On the American continent, the Mexican Indians were cultivating primitive forms of corn from local grasses around 5000 B.C. Its mutations would not reach the southeastern United States until 700 B.C. and the woodlands' southeastern Mississippian cultures around A.D. 900.

THE LATE ARCHAIC PERIOD
4000 to 1000 B.C.

The interaction between the Middle Archaic bands of pre-Algonquian-Muskhogean speakers had resulted in a division of two related yet different tongues. The early versions of the Algonquian language were being spoken throughout the northeastern, Middle Atlantic, Great Lakes, and upper Mississippi Valley woodlands. The early Muskhogean speech bound together the peoples living in all the southeastern woodlands. A common means of communication fostered common cultures and traditions, and by 2000 B.C. the Algonquians had progressed to a mature Algonquian language with its own regional variations in dialect.

About this time the pre-Iroquoians went their separate way with their own speech. These independent Late Archaics ranged from the Lake Erie and the upstate New York areas on into Ontario, Canada. Although very nearly surrounded by Algonquian speaking bands, they would one day become a

HAFTED WITH
TWO SAPLINGS
THINNED AT
THE BEND

CHANNELED
GOUGE

CELT

FULL-GROOVED AXE
—HAFTINGS ARE CONJECTURAL—

24

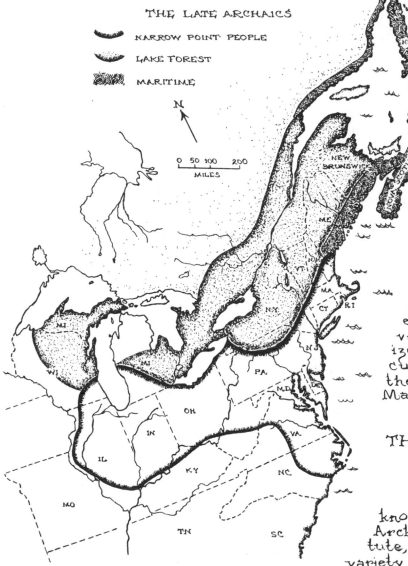

THE LATE ARCHAICS

~ NARROW POINT PEOPLE

LAKE FOREST

MARITIME

formidable threat to their neighbors.

As the Late Archaic period began, the northern Algonquians became the spark plugs for all the rest of their Algonquian brothers and sisters. From their own environment came the innovative ideas that characterized each of the three new cultures ~ the Narrow Point, the Lake Forest, and the Maritime Archaic Peoples.

THE NARROW POINT PEOPLE 4000 to 1000 B.C.

These bands are otherwise known as the Mast Forest Archaics ~ a reasonable substitute, since "mast" recognizes the variety of nuts from the deciduous forest. But the name used here is a hats-off recognition to the inventive spirits in the Merrimack Valley of New Hampshire and their light and efficient thin-bladed points with squared bases. The idea caught on all over most of the Algonquian countryside, where Atlatl darts were bringing down the smaller post~Ice Age game. Although there were some side-notched and early triangular varieties here and there, the narrow small point was preferred along the coast from southern New England down to North Carolina. It spread westward along the southern shores of Lake Erie and Lake Michigan into the Ohio River branches in Illinois, Indiana, and Ohio.

Fishing was competing with hunting as a subsistance mainstay. The Narrow Point People (or Small Point or Mast Forest People, if you wish) along the coast are remembered for their extensive fish weirs. The famous Boylston Street weir was uncovered during the excavation of the Boston subway system in 1913. Stakes measured between 4 to 6 feet in length and 2½ inches in diameter had been sharpened and driven

MERRIMACK

into the tidal flats. (In Late Archaic times the sea level was 16 feet lower than it is today and gradually rose with the glacial meltoffs.) Thousands of sapling poles formed one or more circles of some 200 feet in diameter. The poles were interwoven with branches and brush, and a woven, funnel-shaped entrance faced the current. High tide did the work by bringing in the catch, which could then be easily netted or speared as the tide lowered

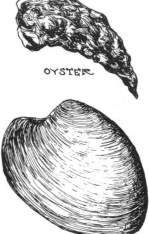
OYSTER

QUAHOG

Shellfish offered a welcome change of diet. Oysters were the favorites all along the coast, yet a pound provided but 400 calories. One of the best known shell middens (groupings of shell heaps) was, of all places, at the Hudson River estuary. Oysters thrived there, measuring up to 10 inches in diameter, because of the river's freshwater flow. A mixture of freshwater and saltwater with a salinity of 22 parts per thousand, instead of the ocean's 35 parts per thousand, certainly made for happy oysters. Coastal quahogs (hard-shell clams), soft shell clams, periwinkles, Ark shellfish, and the more southerly Atlantic ribbed mussels were there for the digging. The great shell middens still stands as monuments to Indian tastes from the Early Archaic days. Most are now protected against those who would level them for use as agricultural fertilizer.

SOFT-SHELL CLAM

PERIWINKLE

We know little about the Narrow Point people's art, ornamentation, and magical or religious beliefs. There is evidence that the scattered Late Archaic bands with family ties and similar interests were joining together as villagers. We also have solid information about how their dwellings appeared. Dating back to 2300 B.C., the Wapanucket site was discovered on the shore of Assowompsett Pond in Plymouth County, Massachusetts. A group of seven circular houses were arranged in two parallel arcs. One, probably a ceremonial building, was 66 feet in diameter. The remaining houses ranged between 30 and 45 feet in diameter. The post holes that outlined each were in pairs, measured $2\frac{1}{2}$ inches in diameter, and were planted to a depth of 11 inches. They indicated overlapping passage entrances much like a snail's shell, facing away from the prevailing winds. In each of the smaller dwellings would be fifteen to twenty patrilineal family members, all related by blood or marriage.

TURKEY WING ARK SHELL

ATLANTIC RIBBED MUSSEL

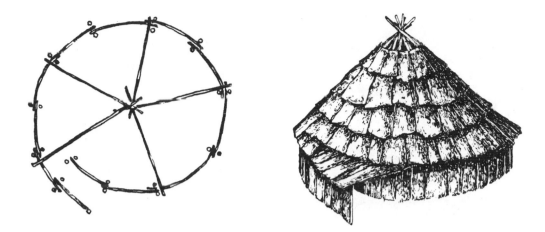

That would bring the total number to one hundred villagers.

THE LAKE FOREST PEOPLE: 3000 to 1000 B.C.

North of the Narrow Point People were fellow Algonquians who lived around the waterways of the St. Lawrence River and the Great Lakes. The birch, oak, walnut, and butternut trees had edged into the lands of the Lake Forest People, just below a belt of solid evergreens in Canada. Since winter came early and stayed late, tracking was often on snowshoes. Here the narrow points never caught on, and atlatl darts were armed with ear-notched and side-notched broad-bladed points.

LAKE FOREST POINTS

Meat ran a second best to freshwater fishing in this water-rich country, for here the Late Archaics were specialists on anything that swam.

The fishhooks and lines used elsewhere had little place among these big-catch people. The men would set out in their dugout canoes with three-pronged bone spears, gaffs with hooked poles to bring the larger fish aboard, and harpoons ready when the occasion demanded. Nearer shore were lengthy gill nets and seines woven from vegetable fibers, all suspended with floats and weighted down with plummets. And of course they were ready for the great spring spawning runs. Their tool kits included ground slate double-edged and crescent-shaped ulus, or knives, for processing their catches. Not all were stone, for the Lake Forest People were most fortunate to have another important natural resource~ copper. Pure copper nuggets had been discovered in the glacial deposits along

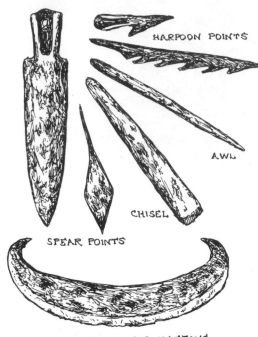

HARPOON POINTS

AWL

CHISEL

SPEAR POINTS

OLD WITH PRONGS FOR HAFTING

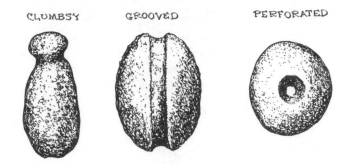

CLUMBSY   GROOVED   PERFORATED

the southern shore of Lake Superior. The mother lode was at Isle Royale, Michigan, and was the heart of this so-called Old Copper Culture. Attempts to pound the soft metal into the same kind of tools that were chipped from stone just didn't work. The hammered copper became brittle and resisted shaping. Trial and error revealed that with repeated heatings, the metal nuggets could be shaped by pounding and intermittent annealing. (Isolated as they were in America, they couldn't know that pure copper could be extracted from its ore through smelting, and the molten metal could then be poured into countless shapes.) The shiny copper tools and ornaments that the Lake Forest craftsmen produced promptly became must-have trade goods among the other Late Archaic villagers.

THE MARITIME PEOPLE: 3200 to 1200 B.C.

Along the North Atlantic coastline lived a third culture that had little in common with the Narrow Point or the Lake Forest People. Indeed, these seagoing northerners seemed to have no ties at all with the Algonquian speakers. It may be that their ancestors were the same Paleo-American hunters who continued their pursuit of cold-loving animals into the sub-Arctic; at least we know they were in place well before the first wave of Eskimos invaded America's northern reaches. They seem to have migrated southward from the Labrador and Quebec shores and spread down along the Gulf of St. Lawrence to Newfoundland, the Maritime Provinces, New Brunswick, and down through Maine as far as the Androscoggin River.

Nothing in North America could compare with the Maritime Archaics' enthusiastic preparations for the life hereafter. Nineteenth-century archaeologists were amazed to find great quantities of a red-stained pigment in their burial sites. They were promptly dubbed the "Red Paint People." This substitute for life-giving blood, red ocher (iron oxide), was carried from central Maine outcrops near the present Katahdin Iron Works. The grave sites, with their telltale red markers, were located on east-facing knolls that overlooked the larger rivers. The acid soil of the northern evergreen forests left little or no evidence of skeletons or of wood, leather, or woven fibers. From the scanty findings it would appear that those who died in the winter were disarticulated, bundled, and placed in temporary shallow graves. With the spring thaws, they could be interred in cemeteries with the proper ceremonial rites along with more recent corpses, which were left intact.

When it came to grave offerings, the Maritime People pulled out all the stops. There were magical quartz crystal charms and amulets of mammal teeth and claws for successful hunts in the spirit world. There were stylistic whale and porpoise effigies along with carved bone and antler decorations. Handsome bayonetlike spearheads of smoothly ground slate, fragile and impractical for this world, would be appropriate for the world beyond. Mystical medical bundles and fire-making kits of iron pyrites and chert would give comfort. There were stemmed points of translucent Labrador quartzite, but no narrow points. Heavy woodworking tools such as axes, adzes, and gouges were of polished green metamorphosed volcanic stone and were accompanied by whetstones for keeping sharply honed edges. Wooden utensils and dug-out canoes could be made if needed. All such prized goods, along with the bloodlike sprinklings of red ocher, were included for all~ male or female, young or old.

This emphasis on one's spiritual well-being would grow and develop throughout most of the woodlands. It began in a more materialistic way when the Maritime Archaic traders brought their works of religious artistry to many far-off villages.

Many of their trips were probably made in dugout canoes. Their fine woodworking tools are evidence of that fact, and their name speaks well for their sea-going adventures. They took seals, walruses, porpoises, and whales with barbed and toggled harpoon heads crafted from bone, antler, and swordfish swords. These they secured temporarily in the harpoon shaft, then freed when the harpoon head had imbedded in the target. The catch was then hauled with the line that was attached to the harpoon head. By dugout they also caught large fish with bone hooks weighted by sinkers. Closer to shore, they they took fish with stationary nets and three-pronged bone fish spears. Surprisingly, the inexhaustible supply of shellfish along the shores was largely ignored.

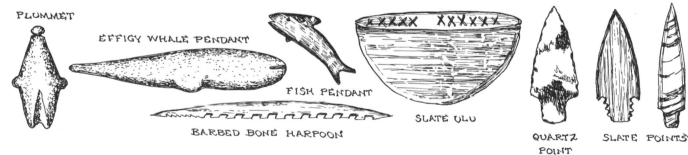

MARITIME ARCHAIC GRAVE GOODS

PLUMMET

EFFIGY WHALE PENDANT

FISH PENDANT

BARBED BONE HARPOON

SLATE ULU

QUARTZ POINT

SLATE POINTS

THE TERMINAL ARCHAIC PERIOD:
2000 to 1000 B.C.

The innovative northeasterners had settled into a satisfying lifestyle. The central and coastal Algonquians were on their way to having common customs and traditions in their tribal villages: The narrow-pointed atlatl dart points were widely used by the Algonquian speakers; trade for the highly valued copper tools and ornaments of the Lake Forest Archaics had encouraged a taste for the luxuries in life; and the missionary enthusiasm and exotic grave goods of the Maritime Archaics focused them on the importance of preparing for life after death. Yet each tribe retained its individuality as dictated by the local environment— climate, topography, river and ocean resources, woodland variations in flora and fauna, and the minerals and workable stones available.

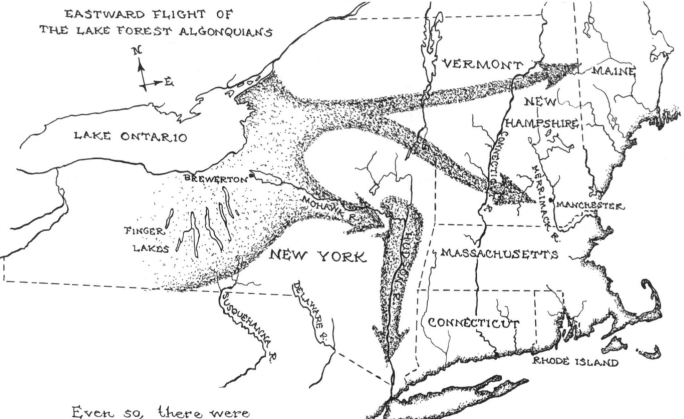

EASTWARD FLIGHT OF
THE LAKE FOREST ALGONQUIANS

Even so, there were unforeseen problems brewing in the woodlands. The pre-Iroquoians were also developing their own way of life, and it was there in the heart of the Lake Forest country that the troubles began. Raids and outright warfare erupted, and at the Brewerton site at New York's Finger Lakes a massacre of some proportions occurred. Archaeologists unearthed a number of male adult skulls with embedded projectile points and fractures. Other skeletons had stone points lodged in their chest cavities. About this time a general upheaval and exodus took place around the trouble spot. The flight was eastward, for at the Neville site in Manchester, New Hampshire, a mixture of narrow points and Lake Forest artifacts have been found. Similar discoveries have been made along the Mohawk and the middle to lower Hudson River drainage— the so-called Vosburg phase.

Other Lake Forest Algonquians were on the move eastward from northern New York, Vermont, and the St. Lawrence River Valley. Distancing themselves from the warring pre-Iroquois, they filtered into the Maritime Archaic lands in the far northeast. By 1880 B.C., the spectacular "Red Paint" burials had completely ceased~ perhaps as a result of the intruding fugitive Lake Forest people. Examples of the heavy woodworking tools that gave the Maritimers their seagoing dugout canoes also disappeared by that date. Wherever they went or whatever their fate, the incoming Algonquians had taken over the old Maritime Archaic haunts.

There is a strong suspicion that the newcomers soon replaced the dugout canoe tradition with a new canoe that was sheathed entirely by white birch bark. With it they could paddle upriver to the deep inland forests for their hunting. They also discovered the rich shellfish reserves that had been ignored by those they had replaced. Maine's huge shell middens give an idea of their taste for these delicacies. The Lake Forest transplants are believed to be the Algonquian ancestors of the Micmac, Maliseet, and Abnaki tribes.

The grave-conscious Maritime People were gone but definitely not forgotten. Although many coastal Algonquians preferred cremation, their grave sites were sprinkled with red-ocher powder in the Maritime tradition. Specially designed grave offerings were also an important part of the burial ritual and were often broken to release the spirit of the bowl or tool for use in the afterworld by the dead's departed spirit. A basic religion would seem well established. The Algonquians believed that all earthly things, living or inanimate, had been given a soul by the Great Spirit.

Not all the Terminal Archaic changes originated in the Northeast. At the start of the period, the Susquehanna River Valley Algonquians had chanced upon the many merits of their local steatite outcroppings. Otherwise known as soapstone, it was found that it was soft enough to be worked into chunky, flat-bottomed pots. First crafted as grave goods, these roughly shaped oval or rectangular pots with lug handles could also serve the living. Not only could they hold a stew or any other liquid, but the soapstone absorbed heat so well that the contents would continue simmering for

31

some time. It's hard to imagine the cooks of today trying to cope in a potless kitchen.

The stone pot invention spread to the coastline and beyond. The steatite quarries in the Carolinas and along Virginia's James and Potomac River Valleys were soon turning out their own labor-saving copies. When word reached southern New England, the tribes there produced a more finished product with smoother sides and rounder bases than the originals.

A SOUTHERN NEW ENGLAND STEATITE BOWL

The Susquehanna People then realized that the versatile soapstone could be worked into gorgets. These pierced decorations were likely worn with thongs about the neck as badges of rank or decoration. For years it had been assumed that they were wrist guards to ward off the sting of a released bowstring, but the bow and arrow would not be used by the Woodland Indians until the beginning of the Late Woodland period in A.D. 700. The atlatl spears were more in use than ever, and the atlatl weights that hurled them were elaborately carved, not surprisingly, of soapstone.

There were other changes in this transitional period. The Susquehannas preferred a thick-stemmed, broad, and heavier atlatl dart point to the earlier stemmed narrow point. Their lengthy cutting edges made them equally useful as knife blades. Others were experimenting with triangular points with concave bases and with still another that was first discovered and named at Orient, Long Island (it had no Asian connections). Found locally in the Hudson River Valley area, the Orient Fishtail point's V-notched stem was a variation of the narrow point. As has been mentioned earlier, changes in hunting points serve as identification markers for archaeologists until the introduction of pottery.

SUSQUEHANNA   ORIENT

The Terminal Archaic Period between 2000 and 1000 B.C. signaled dramatic changes in many parts of the world. The use of bronze had spread throughout Europe; the Eskimo culture began in the Bering Strait area, and man was cultivating rice in the Far East. Horses were tamed and ridden in Central Asia. The invention of ocean-going outrigger canoes permitted travel between the South Pacific Islands. Iron first came into use in the Near East, and the first complete alphabet in script was in use in Syria.

GORGETS

2 EARLY WOODLAND PERIOD
1000 B.C. to A.D. 700

The Maritime religious fever was certainly catching. It spread westward to the eastern and northern New York pre-Iroquois tribes and on to the Lake Forest tribes of Indiana, Ohio, and Michigan. Hotbeds of the Red Paint burials in the Great Lakes areas were the Old Copper and the Glacial Kame Algonquians. The latter tribe earned its name because of the area's small and lumpy hills left by the glaciers.

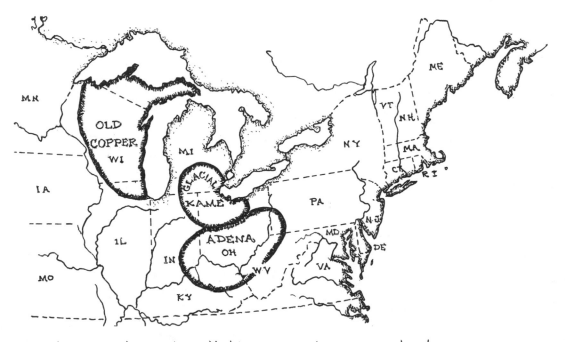

For the most part, all these northern central woodland people had the same mortuary ceremonialism. Most practiced cremation and used a common grave for the burned remains. Red ocher was added as well as occasional unburned local grave offerings. From the Old Copper tribes came the desirable copper tools and ornaments. The Glacial Kame People contributed round and rectangular shell beads from the Great Lakes and the unique "sandal-sole" shell gorgets that probably served as neck ornaments or badges of status. They also buried their dead in the glacial mounds, thereby setting a trend for the Early and Late Woodland grave sites that would follow.

SANDAL-SOLE GORGET

33

THE ADENA MOUND BUILDERS
800 B.C. to A.D. 100

All but the Ohio River drainages in the Narrow Point woodlands had adapted the Maritime concern for the welfare of the dead. It was around 800 B.C. that the Adena Algonquians of southern Ohio took notice of the graveside rituals that had captivated their neighbors. Their enthusiasm reached new heights. Impressed by the Glacial Kame hill burials, they built their own great conical earthen mounds basketful by basketful. The Adenas took the growing preference for cremation one step further. After death, the bodies were defleshed by carrion feeders. The bundled bones were then temporarily laid to rest in a shelter atop one of the mounds. Periodically in a great ceremony, the hut and its contents were set on fire. The Adenas then covered the remains with red ocher and basketfuls of earth, adding yet another layer to the skyward buildup.

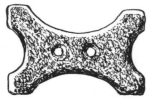

REEL-SHAPED GORGET

ADENA BIRD DESIGN TABLET

Not every Adena would find a resting place in the common grave mound. More important people, such as priests, village leaders, and the well-to-do, would be laid out in log-lined or clay-faced pockets within smaller and more exclusive mounds. Instead of being cremated their bodies would be smeared with the life-giving red iron ocher. Their VIP treatment would include such fine grave offerings as 3-x-4-inch tablets engraved with stylistic birds or geometric designs that may have memorialized the status of the departed. That seems likely, for the tablets had sharpening grooves for the bone tattooing awls that accompanied them. The awls were used to prick permanent skin designs to signify one's social position. Reel-shaped and shell gorgets may also have been worn as decorations of rank.

For the practicalities of the spiritual world, there might be finely crafted boat- and bird-shaped stone atlatl weights and turkey-tail projectile points. The ceremonial use of tobacco had reached the Adenas by this time, and a tubular pipe for smoking would be included. There would be such perishables as cloth, sandals, cordage, torches, wooden bowls, and gourd utensils. Apparently the cremated common folk could do without such spiritual advantages.

In addition to the burial mounds, there were other, more puzzling earthworks known as "sacred circles." These were great circular trenches, dug to provide enough dirt for the surrounding earthen walls. The enclosures averaged a sizable 300 feet in diameter and were perforated by occasional entrance gaps. Sometimes a burial mound was built within one of these circles, but we know not why.

The Adena enthusiasm for elaborate burials spread to the far-reaching Algonquian tribes, and the demand for their artistic grave offerings was great. From the heart of the Adena lands at Chillicothe, Ohio, came traders ready to exchange their

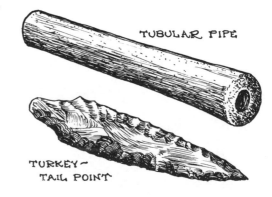

TUBULAR PIPE

TURKEY-
TAIL POINT

goods for unusual raw materials. They set up trading posts in nearby. Indiana, southwestern Pennsylvania, and northern Kentucky. From these outposts, they covered the distances to the Chesapeake Bay area, New Jersey, New England, and New York. Although the mound-building concept never caught on in the more distant reaches, the unusual grave articles were highly prized.

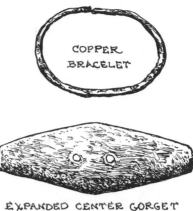

COPPER BRACELET

EXPANDED CENTER GORGET

These trader-missionaries served another important function, for they spread the word about the latest Early Woodland advances. More will be said of the important introductions of clay pottery and of the cultivated gardens that dominated the Early and Late Woodland Periods. It wasn't long before Vinette I pottery had made the soapstone bowl industry obsolete. Because these everyday cooking pots were so commonplace, they were not included in the mound burials.) The Adena travelers also told of their efforts to cultivate plants instead of foraging for wild edibles. The tubular clay pipes and gourd containers they introduced hint of these early crops. All in all, these southern Ohio Algonquians made lasting impressions in those Early Woodland days.

BOATSTONE

BIRDSTONE

THE HOPEWELL MOUND BUILDERS
300 B.C. to A.D. 400

It would seem that the energetic mound-building thrust was finally running out of steam, sputtering to a stop shortly after 100 B.C. After a two-hundred-year rest, though, the southern Ohioans were back with a second wind, ready to build on their earlier successes. They were the same go-getters with a new name to mark the new momentum. Their influences were so far-reaching that some archaeologists have placed them in a separate Middle Woodland Period.

Although the burial sites hadn't changed all that much, the mounds were certainly larger and more imposing than ever before. But what really made the Adena/Hopewell peoples worthy of their important place in our prehistory books was the superb craftsmanship of their trade and burial goods. From their workshops in the Chillicothe area came intricately shaped stone platform pipes surmounted with effigy birds, animals, and human forms. There were polished rectangular stone gorgets; pearl beads; fanciful engravings on copper, wood, and bone; and clever mica cutout designs. From copper nuggets came wrought celts, axes, gouges, ear spoons, breast and head ornaments, and pan pipes. There were also wonderfully chipped obsidian ceremonial knives.

This time around the trade routes extended from the Atlantic seaboard clear to the western Rocky Mountains. No distance was too great for the Hopewell traders in the search for new and unusual raw materials. They were returning with western obsidian, copper and silver nuggets, mica, soapstone, graphite, quartz crystals, galena from lead ore, seashells, pearls, and even shark, barracuda, and alligator teeth. The trading missionaries now concentrated on their neighbors in Illinois, Wisconsin, and beyond the Mississippi River into Iowa.

Then it was on to the untapped possibilities to the south. Somehow these Ohio Algonquians were able to deal with the Muskhogean speakers in Louisiana, Alabama, Tennessee, the Florida Gulf Coast, and Georgia— perhaps through their common roots in the early pre-Algonquian Muskhogean language.

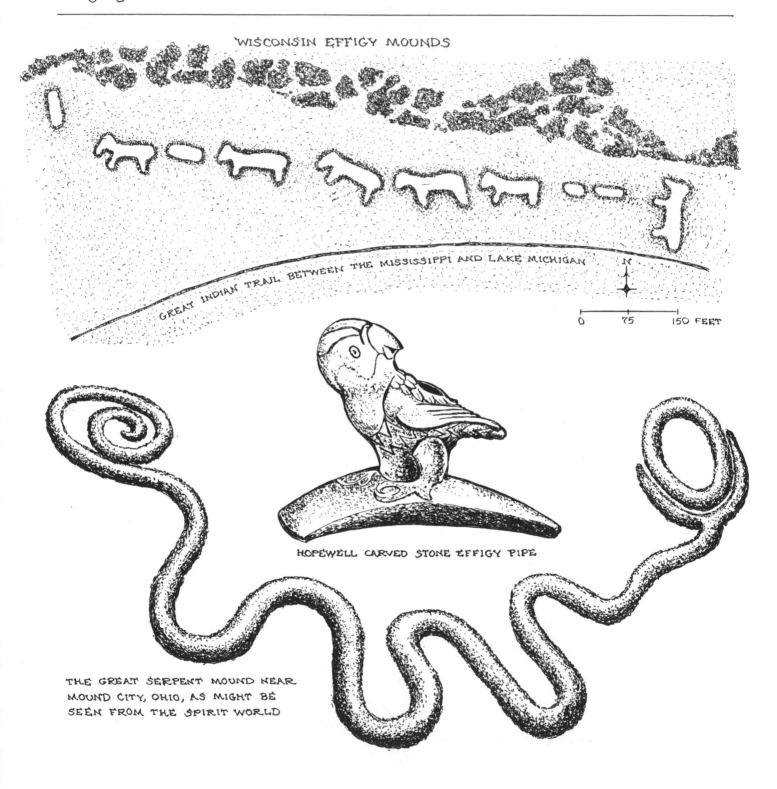

WISCONSIN EFFIGY MOUNDS

GREAT INDIAN TRAIL BETWEEN THE MISSISSIPPI AND LAKE MICHIGAN

N

0   75   150 FEET

HOPEWELL CARVED STONE EFFIGY PIPE

THE GREAT SERPENT MOUND NEAR MOUND CITY, OHIO, AS MIGHT BE SEEN FROM THE SPIRIT WORLD

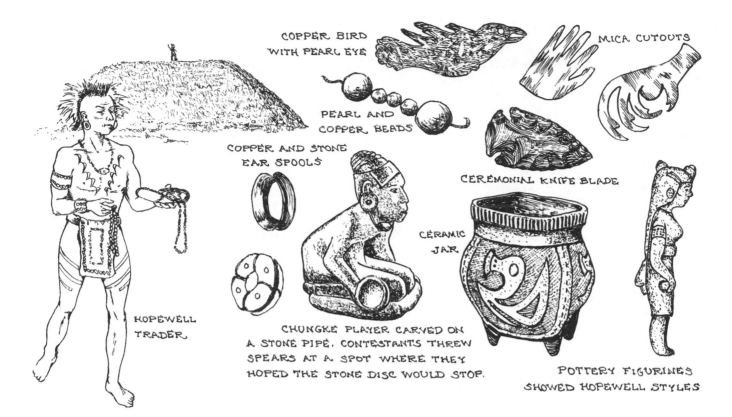

COPPER BIRD WITH PEARL EYE

MICA CUTOUTS

PEARL AND COPPER BEADS

COPPER AND STONE EAR SPOOLS

CEREMONIAL KNIFE BLADE

CERAMIC JAR

HOPEWELL TRADER

CHUNGKE PLAYER CARVED ON A STONE PIPE. CONTESTANTS THREW SPEARS AT A SPOT WHERE THEY HOPED THE STONE DISC WOULD STOP.

POTTERY FIGURINES SHOWED HOPEWELL STYLES

The raw materials taken in trade were funneled back to the workshops. The old favorites of the Hopewell's Adena forefathers ~ the reel-shaped and shell gorgets and the engraved tablets ~ were still being crafted. Far more important was the grave pottery that will be described shortly under the Early Woodland ceramics section.

Wealth and prestige were again flowing into the Hopewell villages. The entrepreneurs involved in the extensive life-after-death network might be called North America's first capitalists. Priests, chieftains, councilmen, craftspeople, tradesmen, and middlemen had risen above the average villager. They could boast of larger dwellings for their families and relatives and afford the good things of life that their status required. Family members could point with pride to such exalted male or female blood relations, and here may very well have been the beginnings of the tribal clans. Membership could only come through blood birth or intermarriage. It did not matter whether the connection was patrilineal or matrilineal. A trader's wealth would guarantee one of the individual mound graves and a swift, direct route to the spirit world.

Nothing succeeds like success. The burial mounds were becoming more spectacular than ever. One of the most notable was raised southwest of Mound City, Ohio. There an earthen serpent still twists along a hilltop for nearly a mile. It begins with an oval mound clamped between great jaws and ends with a huge coiled tail. Such wonders were so admired that new and curious mound shapes would be created in many areas of strong Hopewell influence. The Hopewell's fellow Algonquians on the coastal side of the Appalachian Mountains, however, seemed to shrug off such ostentatious displays. Only the pre-Iroquoians in that area built their own modest mortuary mounds, and thereafter they would be influenced by many other customs to their south.

EARLY WOODLAND CERAMICS

The Early Woodland Period came into being with the introduction of pottery making and the cultivation of gardens. Although not the originators, the Adena / Hopewell people were instrumental in spreading the word throughout the woodland area.

The natives of Georgia first experimented with clay pot-making as early as 2500 B.C., but the general acceptance and use of ceramics in the woodlands came between 1000 B.C. and A.D. 1000. During that time the first efforts produced a chunky copy of the then-popular soapstone bowl. Through trial and error the Early Americans found that modeled clay would shrink and crack when dried or when heated over a fire. They solved the problem by mixing in particles of Spanish moss or some such organic fiber, which also made the pots more durable. Many years down the pottery path, other Woodland Indians realized that inorganic materials such as stones and burned shells made an excellent temper when crushed.

By 1350 B.C. Mexico's pre-Mayan Indians were turning out rather artistic pottery along with a variety of quaint figures. In Susquehanna country to the north, the Algonquians along the Potomac River drainage and coastal New Jersey were shaping their own soapstone bowl look-alikes in clay. The soft steatite could be easily pulverized as temper, and there was certainly plenty of it now that the heavy, labor-intensive stone pots were out of date.

MAYAN FIGURINE
PLAYING PANPIPES

It was about 1000 B.C. when the pottery idea made believers of the Long Island Indians of New York. They developed the technique of laying coil upon coil of pliable clay, thereby producing a thinner, lighter, and well-shaped result. The coiled layers were then thinned further inside and outside with a cord-wrapped paddle to a thickness of but $\frac{1}{3}$ to $\frac{1}{2}$ inch. The tiny cord impressions gave a greater heating surface and a faster boil for the stew pot. The result was the much-copied Vinette I design with straight sides that were sometimes flared at the rim. Its cone-shaped bottom could be set securely into the earthen hearth before a fire was built around its sides.

CHECKERBOARD
WOODEN PADDLE

CONJECTURAL

VINETTE I

CORD-WRAPPED-
STICK MARKS

Word of the new efficient design quickly spread to the north and south, but it would take four hundred more years before the Woodland Indians west of the Appalachian Mountain barrier caught up with the rest. It was then that the Adena craftspeople added their own touch to the Vinette I design by impressing a checkerboard pattern with the carved face of a wooden paddle. The check-stamping became the rage in the southern woodlands~

so much so that it became their own identification characteristic.
This touch of artistry wasn't enough to place this common ware on the Adena "must" list of grave-goods-ultimates. It remained for their Hopewellian descendants to raise the humble baked-clay pot to new heights. To a globular pot designed exclusively for mortuary use, the Hopewells often added four symmetrical bulges by pressing a rounded bone against the inner walls. Geometric and birdlike designs were added and then highlighted with a toothed "rocker stamper" for a zigzag background. By A.D. 250 this rocker-stamping method had been widely adopted by western and northeastern Woodlands Indians to set off their own local designs.

A POSSIBLE ROCKER STAMPING TOOL ~ A NOTCHED SHELL

Probably the most distinctive and admired examples of clay artistry from this period were the Hopewell figurines. Beautifully detailed, these small statues of both men and women give an accurate, three-dimensional picture of the Hopewell people and their tastes in dress and ornaments. Later the upcoming Temple Mound Builders in the Late Woodland southeast would dazzle any viewer with their ceremonial bowls that projected birds and effigy heads from the rims. These pottery one-of-a-kinds were decorated with a colorful Mayan-inspired negative glazing. More on this oppressive culture shortly, but with all the diversity of pottery design throughout the Early and Late Woodland Periods, there is little wonder that projectile points lost out to the individualistic pottery styles as a means of identifying a tribe and its period.

EARLY WOODLAND
CULTIVATED GARDENS

The introduction of the stone hoe represents the beginning of gardening. The taming of plants was no overnight happening. It wasn't until 500 B.C. that the idea of cultivating wild edibles that had been foraged finally took hold in the woodland villages. Such early transplants included the sunflower (*Helianthus annuus*), lamb's-quarter (*Chenopodium album*), marsh elder or sumpweed (*Iva annuus macrocarpa*), maygrass (*Phalrais caroliniana*), giant ragweed (*Ambrosia trifidia*), knotweed (*Polygonum sp.*), and pigweed (*Amaranthus sp.*) Most of these would end up on the weedpile of today's gardens.

COMMON SUNFLOWER   LAMB'S QUARTER   MARSH ELDER   GIANT RAGWEED

Well before this time, Mexican Indians had been experimenting with the native plants that favored the year-round warmth of their area. As early as 5500 B.C. summer squash, pumpkin, and gourds had been domesticated. By 3000 B.C. the kidney bean had joined their list of good foods along with a primitive form of corn grown from a now extinct local grass: Eight rows of kernels were well protected by a husk wrapping.

The Adenas and their Early Woodlanders had long lived in small and separate villages of no more than four or five dwellings to avoid overforaging for wild roots, seeds, and fruits. It had taken a considerable time for the Mexican hot-weather crops to be at home in the cooler woodlands. Finally, a bit before 700 B.C., the Adenas were cultivating their own squash as well as a few local offerings, such as sunflowers. Corn was a latecomer because of the climate differential. Not until a hardier variety was grown~ probably in the cooler Guatemala Mountains ~ were the Hopewell people able to cultivate a limited crop. Thereafter, such varieties as Northern flint, Flour, and Sweet corn could mature in the shorter and sometimes nippy growing seasons of the northern woodlands, well before the warm-loving squash and beans could be harvested.

There was one crop that was destined for the pipe bowl instead of the cooking bowl~ tobacco. The woody plant originated in South America and by 1000 B.C. had made its way to the Eastern Woodlands by way of the West Indies or the Gulf of Mexico. The *Nicotiana rustica* leaves were smoked by the Woodland Indians as part of the sacred burial rites when they communicated with the supernatural world. Generally, portions of other dried plants, such as sumac leaves and dogwood bark, were added to the tobacco, which, by the way, wasn't the same tobacco the Virginia colonists exported to Mother England. Theirs was a different West Indian variety, *N. tabacum*.

THE PRE-IROQUOIS PATHWAYS

As with all good things, the Adena~ Hopewell era ended quietly. The curious effigy mounds and class distinctions remain puzzles with many a piece still missing. As their influence faded, the pre-Iroquoians in the New York State region began to build a culture of their own. Any tendencies toward the more

KNOTWEED

PIGWEED

BEFORE 5000 B.C.
WILD GRASS

BEFORE 4000 B.C.

1000 B.C.

MAIZE DEVELOPMENT IN
SOUTH-CENTRAL MEXICO

spectacular burial mounds died out, and the tribes reverted to the moundless graves. They discarded the cremation rituals but continued the Hopewellian intact and positioned burials for more important personages. The pre-Iroquoians mostly practiced bundle burials. The bones were buried after the body was defleshed or the soft body tissues were allowed to decay. The Hopewell flavor continued in their straight tubular and platform pipes, but the newly created elbow pipe would become characteristic of Iroquoian design.

ELBOW PIPE

BEFORE A.D. 1000

Of far greater importance was the Hopewell's gardening know-how, and by A.D. 500 the cultivation of plants was providing more food for pre-Iroquoian clay pots than hunting or fishing. The pre-Iroquois had begun to clear land intensively for garden plots. Handy to the growing cultivated acreage were larger, more permanent villages; related families had given up their scattered foraging and hunting camps for a new togetherness. These changes were evident in the Kipp Island and Hunter Home sites collectively known as the Point Peninsula Sequence, between A.D. 800 to 1000.

CLEARING THE LAND FOR GARDENING

The outside world had innovations of its own during the Early Woodland Period. Reindeer were domesticated in northern Europe, the Phoenicians had developed the modern alphabet, the Celts were spreading the use of iron throughout Europe, and the first highway system was built in Assyria.

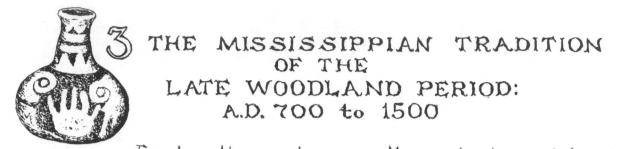

3 THE MISSISSIPPIAN TRADITION
OF THE
LATE WOODLAND PERIOD:
A.D. 700 to 1500

For two thousand years the most advanced American Indian civilizations had centered in Mexico. The Mayans had to their credit the development of cultivated gardens and their uniquely shaped, polychrome pottery, including intricate statuettes. They created ambitious stone carvings, cut-stone bridges and aqueducts, vapor baths, a calendar based on astronomical deductions and even a written language that used symbols for words. It is regrettable that the North American tribes had no such means to record their history through the ages.

Mayan life centered around the Indians' towering stone pyramids, which were capped by temples, and ceremonial plazas. Their civilization depended on the oppressive caste system that made such wonders possible. Yet by A.D. 650 the whole culture was in shambles. Armed mobs of have-nots from the surrounding highland villages were after their piece of the Mayan pie. Great centers such as Teotihuacan were sacked and reduced to piles of rubble.

Perhaps it was the privileged refugees who brought the remnants of their glory days to the Mississippi River Valley. Before long the Hopewellian burial mounds were overshadowed by great earthen pyramidal temple mounds that studded the Mississippi bottomlands from Louisiana to Iowa. Because of the dearth of stones for cutting in the Mayan manner, impressed commoners labored mightily to bring their basketfuls of dirt for each construction. Through such effort, three main centers were created. One was situated in the central Mississippi

A MAYAN PRIEST
POTTERY FIGURINE A.D. 600~900
MUSEUM OF THE AMERICAN INDIAN,
HEYE FOUNDATION

MAYAN TEMPLES SUCH AS EL CASTILLO INSPIRED THE MISSISSIPPIAN TEMPLE MOUNDS.

42

CAHOKIA FLINT HOE WITH POSSIBLE HAFTING

Valley where it merged with the Ohio River. A second was at the headwaters of the Tennessee River, and the last was along the great Red River bend. Understandably, the Mississippians' culture is known as the Temple Mound Culture.

The fertile river silt combined with a kindly climate, enabling the tribes to produce the Mayan-inspired corn, beans, squash, pumpkins, and gourds; South American tobacco; and the more local sunflower and pigweed. There was no need for extensive forest growth clearings along these flat floodplains, and cultivation required little more than a chipped flint hoe. Fish and freshwater mussels were in abundance, and game was never very far away in the woodlands that rimmed the river valleys. The many waterways allowed for communication, travel, and trade between the growing numbers of Temple Mound cities. In short, it was an ideal setting to start a transplanted Mayan lifestyle in the southern woodlands.

THE FASCINATION FOR ALL THINGS MAYAN

Of all the Mississippian Temple Mound cities, none were more awe-inspiring than Cahokia in Illinois. By A.D. 1000, its $3\frac{1}{2}$ square miles near today's East St. Louis was the home of some twenty-thousand people. Along the flatlands were orderly streets lined with wattle and daub buildings, which surrounded large ceremonial plazas. One such central square held the largest mound in all North America. This was the massive Monks' Mound, named for a group of Trappist monks who lived on the truncated pyramid's flat top back in colonial days. The earthwork covered over sixteen acres and rose skyward for 100 feet. In the Temple Mound days, its tablelike top held a 45-X-100-foot wooden building that probably served as the area's principal temple. Atop lesser mounds were the dwellings of important chieftains and their families. The scattered conical mounds

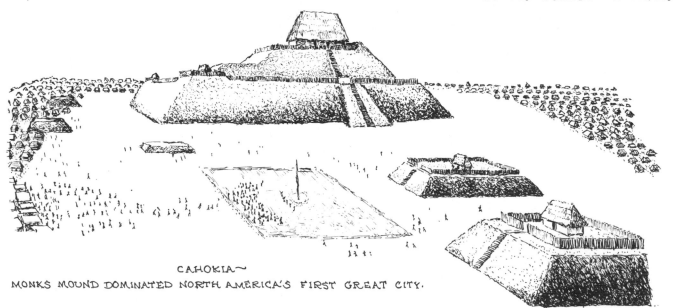

CAHOKIA~
MONKS MOUND DOMINATED NORTH AMERICA'S FIRST GREAT CITY.

were reserved for such VIP burials. Cahokia, by the way, is one of only sixteen sites that have been placed in the World Heritage Site Registry.

Early eighteenth-century French eyewitnesses have removed much of the guesswork about the Mississippian culture. Particularly vivid are their writings about the Natchez tribe living in the southernmost part of the Mississippi Valley. Since the Mississippians were near Mexico and its influences, the caste system had its firm and heavy-handed grip on them. At the top of the caste pyramid was the "Great Sun," the matrilineal descendant of that all-powerful sun god of the sky. A perpetual fire was kept burning in the temple, for the fire, too, was the earthly copy of the sun and it's warmth. Should it ever go out, the Great Sun would perish, and its a sure bet that the "Keeper of the Flame" and his family would meet the same fate at the hands of the high priests. By virtue of his divine powers, this absolute ruler could have any of his subjects killed at his pleasure. He was so exalted that he was not allowed to touch the common ground. Instead, he was carried on a litter or walked on a royal mat, rolled out before him.

le transport du Grand Soleil

ARTIST DU PRATZ SKETCHED THE GREAT SUN BEING CARRIED TO A HARVEST FESTIVAL.
NATCHEZ, 1758   AMERICAN ETHNOLOGY, SMITHSONIAN

When a Great Sun died, it was a certainty that his court would serve him in the spirit world. Early French settlers recorded that, after his death, his wives and household attendants stood on a specially raised scaffold on the plaza, occasionally descending to dance together. After several days had passed, they would be strangled by their closest relatives. The bodies of the Great Sun and his wives were then carried to the temple over a path strewn with strangled infants. The sacrificed bodies were then either buried or cremated, and the bones of the Great Sun would be laid to rest by the temple's eternal flame.

Next in line in this caste system was the Great Sun's brother, Little Sun. He served as the powerful Great War Chief during the period recorded by the French. The Noble class followed, with its assortment of village chieftains, priests, and others of high rank. Then came the Honored, a rank that even the most lowly could aspire to by taking an enemy scalp or performing some similar act of wartime bravery or through a sacrifice. For example, a common family could reach this social level by sacrificing a child upon the death of the Great Sun. An artisan might also be granted such a

VALLEY POT, LOWER MISSISSIPPI

VALLEY POT, CENTRAL MISSISSIPPI

status because of his or her unusual talents in the crafting of pottery, shell carvings, stone work, embossing copper, or fine weaving.

Last and certainly least were the work-horses of Natchez society, the Commoners. They were also known as the Stinkards by those of superior rank. In their day-to-day survival, the women turned out utilitarian pottery with flared rims and loop handles. They minded the house and children, cultivated the fields, dressed hides, or wove clothing and mats. Their husbands made their everyday tools and the weapons for hunting or took their place in the war parties.

The earlier Hopewell clan system idea seemed to fit nicely into this class structure. In the Muskhogean-speaking southeastern regions, the clans were matrilineal~ that is, a person's descent was traced through the mother's line. Therefore the Great Sun was born into his ex-alted position because his mother was the oldest sister of the previous ruler, despite his having a Commoner father. This surprising elevation of a lowly Stinkard to such a lofty position resulted from the iron-clad law that all upper classes, both men and women, must marry Commoners. Its purpose was well con-ceived, for it did keep a varied and healthy gene bank in effect. Since children inherited their mother's class, only a Noble mother could have a noble offspring. But if a child was born of a Commoner mother, he or she would be demoted to one rank lower than that of the father's.

The chilling aspects of the Mayan-adopted culture in the Mis-sissippi Valley~ and throughout the Southeast, for that matter~ did have its lighter moments. There were seasonal celebrations that filled the town and city plazas. The priests officiated in their feathered finery, and it would be a rare onlooker who wasn't impressed by their pomp and splendor. Each new moon brought a new and different observance.

Best known was the Green Corn Ceremony in July or August, after the main crop of corn was harvested. It was also the time when the southeastern New Year began, a time to discard old practices that might be displeasing to the gods. To symbolize this fresh start, the Indians threw out worn clothing and worn-out tools and utensils. The entire town was swept and scoured until it sparkled~ no doubt by the Common-ers. All household fires were snuffed out and then rekindled from a fresh sacred fire that burned in each plaza. Fasting, purging with a black emetic from the Yaupon holly, and ritual bathings would follow. This New Year celebration was of such importance that all sins and crimes excepting murder were pardoned. It was also a time when unmarrieds had complete

SOUTHEASTERN DWELLINGS GENERALLY HAD WALLS OF UP-RIGHT POLES INTERWOVEN WITH BRANCHES AND PLASTERED WITH CLAY. THEY WERE CAPPED WITH GABLED ROOFS OF THATCH.

CENTER— MISSISSIPPIAN HEARTLANDS
DARK PERIPHERY — AREAS GREATLY
    INFLUENCED BY MISSISSIPPIAN CULTURE
LIGHT PERIPHERY — AREAS UNDER LESS
    MISSISSIPPIAN INFLUENCE

sexual freedom. There would also be games of chunky, played with rolling stones and throwing sticks, as well as lacrosse. The Green Corn New Year's ceremonies were celebrated for four to eight days, depending on the size of the town or city.

THE MISSISSIPPIAN SOUTHEASTERN COLONIES

The Mayanization of the Mississippi Valley had been a success from its very beginning. Upper class leaders soon controlled the valley's stone quarries, salt mines, and probably trade and travel over the waterways. But there were other, greater opportunities for the taking all along the many rivers that interlaced the rest of the Southeast. On foot or by canoe, waves of Mississippian colonists invaded the territories still under Hopewell influence. They began their conquest of the Tennessee River and its tributaries, then moved southward into Tennessee, Georgia, and Alabama. Although the invaders were underwhelmed by warm welcomes — the locals were downright hostile — the colonial toeholds in the Southeast persisted and flourished.

These conquests were made possible by the club- and axe-wielding rawhide shield-carrying Mississippian warriors. These aggressive forces also carried the new bow and arrow weapons. The first Eskimo arrivals had introduced them to northern America around 3000 B.C. Between A.D. 400 and 700 the bow and arrow were finally in the hands of the Woodland Peoples. Because decent flint for small triangular points was not easily obtained in the woodlands, they hafted their arrows with a variety of points made from antlers, turkey-cocks' bone spurs, and the teeth of large fish or animals. Woodland bows were longbows — up to 5½ feet long among the Iroquois and the Coastal Algonquians. The southeastern bows were generally shorter and the bows of western tribes ever more so.

An attack by the southeastern warriors was no spur-of-the-moment adventure. As an example, the Caddo warriors of Arkansas and Louisiana prepared for war for nearly a

WITH THE COMING OF THE BOW AND ARROW ABOUT A.D. 700, THE SIDE-NOTCHED AND THE CORNER-REMOVED ATLATL POINTS SERVED AS MODELS FOR THE SMALLER ARROW POINTS. THEY WERE GRADUALLY REPLACED DURING THE LATE WOODLAND PERIOD WITH TRIANGULAR POINTS HAVING CONCAVE OR STRAIGHT BASES.

week. Enlistment feasts, dances, ceremonials,
and rituals were powerful inducements for any who
wavered on joining the glory path to war. And to repeat,
a Commoner who risked his neck— or rather his scalp—
in battle might be granted the Honored title. He would
return home with his own scalp trophies, to the admiration of the village folk. He might also return with an
enemy prisoner who could be adopted (for example, a
Caddoan widow) or readied for torture.

   The prisoner would be forced to dance and sing
in the plaza for several days in front of the crowd of
onlookers. Then the victim would learn about the
Mayan-inspired human sacrifices firsthand. Lashed to
a framework, he would be tortured by fire and then
eaten in a prescribed ritual. No doubt this scene was
a familiar one as the Mississippian colonists continued
their subjugation of the southeastern woodlands.

   Each Mississippian town grew in size and influence. There would certainly be one or more impressive
earthen truncated pyramids with a temple or the dwelling
of a member of the ruling class perched on top. The
plaza would be surrounded by orderly rows of thatched
gable roofs. The walls of these houses were upright poles
interwoven with flexible withes, or canes. There were
colorful ceremonies, and the outstanding Mayan-Missis-
sippian objects crafted out of shell, stone, wood and
ceramics were used in those gatherings. In short, each
colonial town was a mini-reproduction of the splendid Mississippian versions back home. A local visitor couldn't
help but be impressed by the grandeur of it all.

THE SOUTHERN CULT

   All the southeastern woodland Indians had come
around to a somewhat grudging admiration for the Temple

Plan du Fort   Prisonier au Cadre.

SKETCH BY ARTIST DU PRATZ SHOWING TORTURE PREPARATIONS BY NATCHEZ WARRIORS

Mound culture. They were already familiar with the earlier burial mounds of the Adena Hopewells, and the transition was relatively smooth. They added their own symbolic motifs of sun, fire, wind, and human sacrifice to a wide range of ceremonial objects with skill and imagination. There were small copper masks of a long-nosed god. In the Tennessee Cumberland country, striking stone deities nearly 2 feet in height were shaped in various positions. Fine effigy pipes were crafted from stone, and ceremonial one-piece axes, maces, and sacrificial knives were painstakingly chipped from single pieces of flint. Embossed copper sheets featured heroic warriors bedecked in feathered headdresses and holding daggers, decapitated human and bird heads, and similar themes of human sacrifice and death. Gulf shell gorgets, cups, and bowls were engraved with such ritualistic motifs as trilobed arrows and eyes that were winged, forked, weeping, or held in the palm of the hand. Crosses and sunbursts were popular designs.

Pottery had risen to new heights for the southeastern religious rituals. The typical Mississippian ceramic bowls projected human and bird effigy heads from the rims. Because these ceremonial pieces were ornamental and never utilitarian, they were often negatively painted, using a Mexican-inspired technique. First a basic color was applied. Then designs in melted wax were painted over the surface, and the pot was glazed with a second color. When fired, the wax melted off to reveal the designs in a basic color against a background of a second glaze. This pottery along with the other ritualistic trappings, have earned the Temple Mound southeasterners the name Southern Cult.

The Southern Cult tribes resembled a patchwork quilt. Their five principal languages spoke of their

BLACK-AND-WHITE NEGATIVELY PAINTED POTTERY WITH A HAND SYMBOL
MOUNDVILLE, ALABAMA

RITUALISTIC STONE PIPE DEPICTS EXECUTIONER CLEAVING THE SKULL OF A HUMAN SACRIFICE. THE $9\frac{3}{4}$-INCH PIPE HAS BOWL ON FIGURE'S BACK.
SPIRO, OKLAHOMA

FROM A SINGLE PIECE OF STONE, A POLISHED CELT $5\frac{1}{2}$ INCHES LONG
MOUNDVILLE, ALABAMA

A POLISHED STONE BOWL HEADED BY A WOOD-DUCK EFFIGY
MOUNDVILLE, ALABAMA

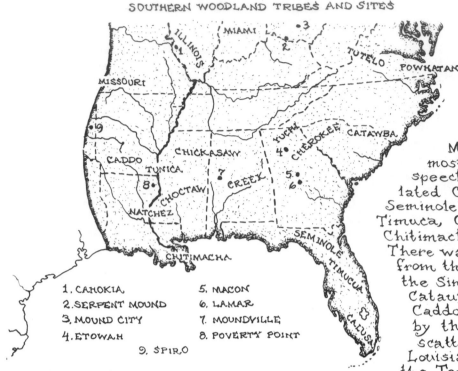

1. CAHOKIA
2. SERPENT MOUND
3. MOUND CITY
4. ETOWAH
5. MACON
6. LAMAR
7. MOUNDVILLE
8. POVERTY POINT
9. SPIRO

diversity. Certainly the Muskhogean tongue was the most widespread and was the speech of the Creek and the related Choctaw, Chickasaw, and Seminole Indians as well as the Timuca, Calusa, Natchez, Tunica, Chitimacha, and Atakapa tribes. There was a scattering of migrants from the Western Plains who spoke the Siouan language — the Tutelo, Catauba, and the Yuchi tribes. Caddo was the tongue of the tribe by that name. Their people were scattered through Arkansas and Louisiana woodlands and over to the Texas border. Still another language, Iroquois, was that of the Cherokee invaders from the north. This tribe had settled into the mountains of North Carolina and neighboring Tennessee.

The Creeks were particularly inspired by the Southern Cult religious movement. They claimed the extensive valley lands along the Tennessee and Cumberland Rivers of western and central Tennessee and on into Georgia. Their name was given to them by English traders who first came upon them by the Ocheese Creek. Their best known Temple Mound cities were near present-day Macon, Augusta, and Savannah. One, the great center of Etowah in northwest Georgia, had one of the largest mounds in all of the southeastern woodlands. It was topped with a temple and surrounded by great plazas, the usual well laid-out streets, and the inevitable stockade. There were always those

SOUTHERN CULT CEREMONIAL SYMBOLS

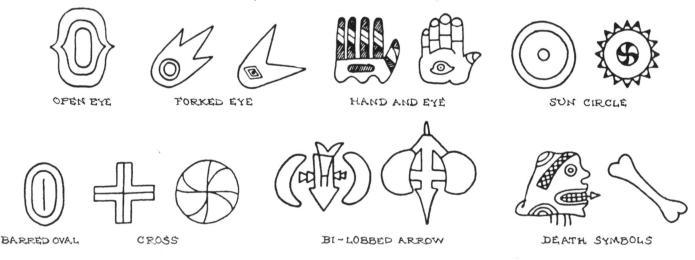

OPEN EYE   FORKED EYE   HAND AND EYE   SUN CIRCLE

BARRED OVAL   CROSS   BI-LOBBED ARROW   DEATH SYMBOLS

envious neighbors and Commoners who would gladly overthrow the privileged classes as they did in the days of the Maya.

Etowah was a woodland wonder, with its large stone sculptures of elderly looking people who may have represented such gods as the Sun and Fire, who had been worshipped in Mexico. There were unusual, boxlike tombs, sided and capped with large stone slabs. The southeastern tribes were so captivated by all such things Mayan that many archaeologists believe the influences must have come directly from the Gulf of Mexico as well as the Mississippi River tribes. Indeed, in 1993, archaeologists discovered the site of El Pital, a Mexican port city of 20,000 souls, whose seagoing trade no doubt included the southeastern and upper Mississippian tribes. Its peak activity was between A.D. 300 and 600.

The Iroquoian-speaking Cherokees were relatively recent arrivals to this Temple Mound country. It was probably during the late Hopewellian period that they migrated through Ohio and displaced those living in the vast Tennessee River Valley. They, too, were caught up in the Mayan culture and have left behind evidence of cultivated gardens, pyramidal mounds and temples, burial rituals, an authoritarian caste system, and artful ceremonial trappings. Yet the Cherokees bypassed the local wattle-and-daub rectangular dwellings in favor of one-door, circular wigwams that may have been an earlier Iroquoian design.

LARGE STONE EFFIGY OF A MAN~ABOUT 1½ FEET TALL ETOWAH, GEORGIA.

EVERYDAY LIFE IN THE SOUTHEASTERN WOODLANDS

We have but sketchy information on the southeastern Woodland Indians, for any of their people who were not destroyed by the series of Spanish invasions were disbanded to Oklahoma by an act of Congress in 1830. From the artifacts they left behind and from a few descriptions recorded by early observers, we can imagine their collective lifestyle to some degree. Day-to-day living was more uneventful than their Temple Mound religious cults would lead us to believe. The agreeable climate permitted successive corn plantings that would end up being roasted green in their husks; added to stews; or dried, ground, and winnowed in sieve baskets. A mixture of the flour and water was baked in ashes as corn bread and hominy was made by soaking kernels in wood-ash lye to remove the hulls. Any surplus corn was stored on the cob in cribs resembling those of later European colonists. Of course there were squash, pumpkin,

RAISED HAMMERED FIGURE OF A PRIEST ON COPPER PLATE FOUND AT THE ETOWAH CEREMONIAL CENTER

50

THE CIRCULAR WALLS OF THE CHEROKEES' DWELLINGS MAY HAVE BEEN WATTLE-AND-DAUB LIKE THOSE OF THE OTHER SOUTHEASTERN TRIBES.

beans, and tobacco crops; seeds from cultivated sunflowers and pigweed; and gourds for containers. There was seasonal foraging for raspberries, mulberries, persimmons, walnuts, acorns, and tubers, which could be dried for later use. Except for the sacred tobacco crop, all were a part of the women's chores.

The river-valley fishermen were expert with hook and line, and woven fish traps. They also waded into the shallow waters of their weirs to take their fish with bows and arrows and blowguns, the projectile points of the latter having been coated with a paralyzing root juice. This same weapon and its small, notched, triangular points were used to bring down bison, bear, deer, turkey, and migrating fowl. This varied menu was available throughout most of the year. The southeasterners could therefore stay put in more permanent dwellings, unlike the seasonal shifts of the Algonquians to the north.

Their appearance wasn't all that different from that of the other Woodland Indians. They had no patience with facial hair and would pluck any offenders that dared surface with bivalve shell tweezers. They took pride in their straight black hair. (Baldness was a rarity.) Although the roach, or center hair strip, was favored by most men, hair was styled according to individual or tribal taste. The Caddo tribe, for example, preferred a crown patch of hair, grown to the waist and embellished with feathers.

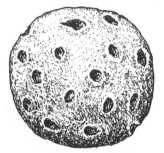

INDENTED BAKED-CLAY BALLS WERE HEATED IN FIRES, THEN PLACED IN POTS OF WATER AND SOUP TO BOIL THE LIQUIDS.

ARTIST JACQUES LE MOYNE CAME TO THE NEW WORLD IN 1564 WITH THE HUGUENOTS. HIS PAINTINGS OF THE FLORIDA NATIVES WERE REPRODUCED IN FORTY-THREE ENGRAVINGS BY THEODORE DE BRY IN 1591.

THIS ENGRAVING IS TITLED "STORING THEIR CROPS IN THE PUBLIC GRANERY."

Tattooing was right in style~ and the more, the better. Even boys and girls of the Natchez tribe were decorated across their respective noses. As one's wealth and position increased through the years, more were added to give something of a pictorial review of the individual's achievements and class standing. These epidermal displays were enhanced by spool earrings and necklaces that had remained in style for both sexes since Hopewellian days.

As elsewhere in the woodlands, the usual dress of the day was a breechclout and moccasins. Any travel through brush and brambles called for protective leggings and shirts. Cooler weather could be met with the insulation provided by a feather or a fur cloak. The air-pocketed fur was worn next to the skin. Women might also wear skirts of soft deerskin or woven grass or the pliable inner bark of trees.

Hernando de Soto's expedition, while zigzagging across the southeast in 1540 and 1541, had only admiration for the native costumes. An expedition member noted, "The skins are well dressed ~ the color being given to them that is wished ~ and in such perfection that when of vermilion they look like very fine red broadcloth; and when black~ the sort used for shoes~ they are of the purest. The same hues are given to blankets."

WINTER WEAR FOR THIS LOUISIANA BRAVE WAS A DECORATED BUFFALO ROBE AND LITTLE ELSE BUT ITS PRIZED TAIL. THE SMALL ANIMAL POUCH MAY BE FOR TOBACCO, TUCKED UNDER THE BREECH BELT WITH A PIPE. BY FRENCH ARTIST ALEXANDER DE BATZ BETWEEN 1732 AND 1735

Giving birth was a do-it-yourself project. An isolated riverside hut was provided for delivering as well as for use during menstrual periods, which were somehow considered a threat, and a danger to the men. Some infants, such as the Natchez, were secured on cradleboards, Mayan fashion, to deform the babes' soft cranial bones in accordance with their social status. When the youngsters were older, the girls learned their household skills from their mothers. Boys were schooled by an elder clansman in competitive games to hone their running, swimming, hunting, survival, and warpath skills. There was considerable emphasis on cooperation. Every tribesman must be considered a brother.

The teen years were a time for sexual freedom. Natchez girls were expected to be free with their sexual favors or run the risk

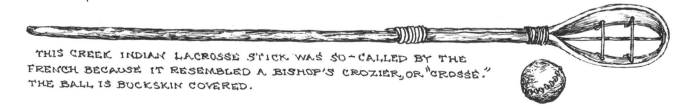

THIS CREEK INDIAN LACROSSE STICK WAS SO-CALLED BY THE FRENCH BECAUSE IT RESEMBLED A BISHOP'S CROZIER, OR "CROSSE." THE BALL IS BUCKSKIN COVERED.

of not being admitted to the spirit world. Marriages were arranged between different clan families; more than two wives was a rarity. Once wedded, there could be no thought of adultery. All in all, there were more similarities than differences among the southeastern woodland peoples. The tribes grew and prospered until the sixteenth-century Spanish conquests.

NORTHERN MISSISSIPPIAN COLONIZATIONS

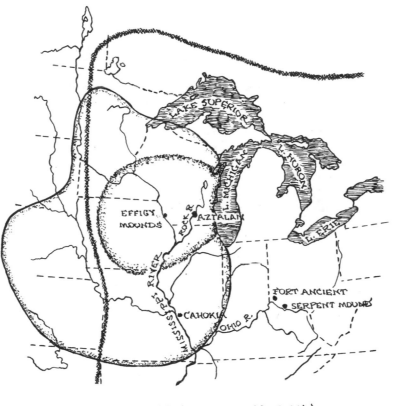

NORTHERN MISSISSIPPIAN COLONIES
WOODLAND BOUNDARY
MIDDLE MISSISSIPPIAN OUTREACH
ONEOTA CULTURE

    The little kings of the Mississippian culture looked to a takeover of the country to the north as well. Settlers set out from the Cahokia area with high hopes of conquering their Wisconsin targets. But the Old Copper and Adena-Hopewell traditions were treasured there, and any hard sell seemed to fall on deaf ears. Still, the downriver colonists did begin to set up their Temple Mound town of Aztalan in southern Wisconsin around A.D. 1000. It was prudent in this unfriendly north to build their twenty-acre foothold by the banks of the Rock River to prevent surprise attacks from that quarter. The remaining three sides of the town featured a high stockade with watchtowers to give notice of any mischief afoot. Long passageway entrances would serve as a trap for any hostile raiders.
Inside, two temple mounds rose above it all. They were a visual proof that the Mississippians were in Wisconsin to stay.
    The Aztalan colonists spoke the Siouan language, a barrier

between them and the local Central Algonquian speakers. But persistence paid off. The Temple Mound influences spread out into other areas of Wisconsin, Illinois, Minnesota, Iowa, Missouri, Kansas, and Nebraska. Collectively, they made up a transitional Oneota culture that combined both Woodland and Plains traditions. The woodland influence was evident in the Hopewellian-style pottery and the occasional animal effigy mounds that remain as reminders of the spectacular serpent earthworks in Ohio. The Aztalan colonial descendants, the Winnebago tribe, still live in the wild rice lake country west of Lake Michigan.

FAILED ATTEMPTS
TO COLONIZE EASTWARD

To the east of the Mississippi Valley and into the extensive Ohio River Valley, any Mississippian push was dead-ended against the Central Algonquian traditions inherited from the Late Archaic Narrow Point, Lake Forest, and Maritime Peoples and their successors, the Adena-Hopewells. This off-limit territory extended from West Virginia to the more westerly Scioto and Miami Rivers. All the villages of this region in the Late Woodland Period have been lumped under the arbitrary name of Fort Ancient Complex.

A flavor of the Temple Mound Culture was evident, however, in the Fort Ancient cultivated floodplain crops, their fortified villages, and bone tools and ornaments. All were overshadowed by the Hopewell-like mounds, some of which contained extended bodies in stone slab-lined vaults, the decorative grave offerings, and the Algonquian-style round, instead of rectangular, wigwams. These villages east of the Mississippi united to become the Shawnee tribe.

SHELL GORGET WITH WOODPECKERS
AND SUN SYMBOL
SPIRO, OKLAHOMA

THE CENTRAL ALGONQUIAN TRIBES

The traditional patterns of life had continued among the Central Algonquian tribes during the Late Woodland Period. Throughout all the radical upheavals in the Southeast, they had remained faithful to the ways of their Late Archaic ancestors and the Adena-Hopewell people. This four-season part of the northcentral woodlands was no place for the permanent Temple Mound cities. The Central Algonquians and their kin, the Coastal Algonquians, still moved in extended family bands during the colder seasons, then came together as a tribe when the warmer planting weather approached. In fall, winter, and spring, these groups would go off on their own for fishing, hunting, and the gathering of wild foods.

TRIBAL ORGANIZATION

Clan membership provided the common bonds connecting the bands of a single tribe. This emphasis on a common ancestor had grown since the days of the Hopewells. They were patrilineal, for the seasonal shifts required that males choose the best hunting and fishing sites, cooperate with other bands, and protect the women and children. While every man was a member of his particular clan by birth, his wife would join his clan by marriage. Their clan names were inspired by wolves, bears, elk, deer, foxes, birds, fish, plants, and even mythical beings. For the most part, the clans were more concerned with the spiritual life beyond the grave than with making political decisions. Perhaps the Adena-Hopewell Burial Mounds influenced them, even if these mobile Algonquians had little use for the spectacular mounds for the dead.

CLAN EMBLEMS

To address the politics of a tribe, two clan divisions representing peace and war acted as decision makers. They were the moieties, otherwise known as "Sky" and "Earth" divisions, among the Winnebago, Menominee, Miami, Illinois, and probably the Kickapoo tribes. The Sky clans, named after the birds of the air and such atmospheric phenomena as thunder, were dedicated to the preservation of peace. Their leader was a tribal chief who was descended from the same bloodline as his predecessors; he

ALGONQUIAN DOME WIGWAM

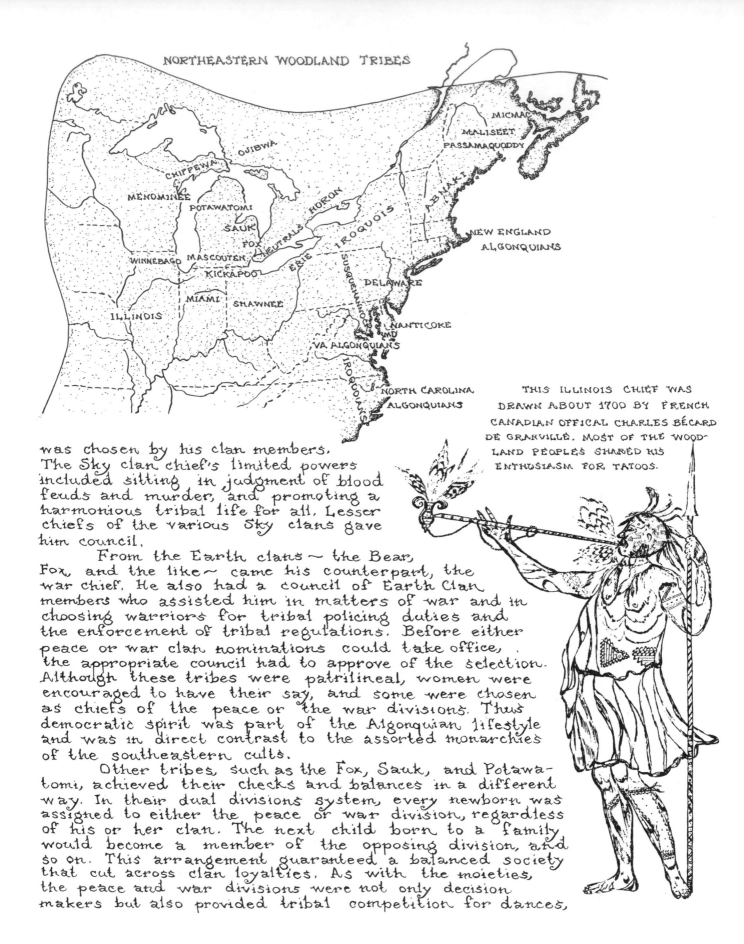

THIS ILLINOIS CHIEF WAS
DRAWN ABOUT 1700 BY FRENCH
CANADIAN OFFICAL CHARLES BÉCARD
DE GRANVILLE. MOST OF THE WOOD-
LAND PEOPLES SHARED HIS
ENTHUSIASM FOR TATOOS.

was chosen by his clan members.
The Sky clan chief's limited powers
included sitting in judgment of blood
feuds and murder, and promoting a
harmonious tribal life for all. Lesser
chiefs of the various Sky clans gave
him council.

From the Earth clans ~ the Bear,
Fox, and the like ~ came his counterpart, the
war chief. He also had a council of Earth Clan
members who assisted him in matters of war and in
choosing warriors for tribal policing duties and
the enforcement of tribal regulations. Before either
peace or war clan nominations could take office,
the appropriate council had to approve of the selection.
Although these tribes were patrilineal, women were
encouraged to have their say, and some were chosen
as chiefs of the peace or the war divisions. Thus
democratic spirit was part of the Algonquian lifestyle
and was in direct contrast to the assorted monarchies
of the southeastern cults.

Other tribes, such as the Fox, Sauk, and Potawa-
tomi, achieved their checks and balances in a different
way. In their dual divisions system, every newborn was
assigned to either the peace or war division, regardless
of his or her clan. The next child born to a family
would become a member of the opposing division, and
so on. This arrangement guaranteed a balanced society
that cut across clan loyalties. As with the moieties,
the peace and war divisions were not only decision
makers but also provided tribal competition for dances,

games, rituals, and warfare training.

To muddy the waters a bit more, the Shawnee tribe had neither moieties nor dual divisions. Because their bands come together as a tribe less often, each was assigned specific tribal political or religious duties for their seasonal reunions in summer and winter. It was then that the tribal chief and his council of band chieftains made decisions of general concern. Such independent and self-sufficient bands ran the risk of going their own way, thereby fragmenting the whole. This seems to have been the fate of the Shawnees, for by the seventeenth century they were scattered throughout Illinois, Maryland, and along the Ohio and Savannah river valleys. Their traditions became diluted as they gradually adapted to the ways of their more unified Delaware, Iroquois, and Creek neighbors.

THE SPIRIT WORLD

The Central Algonquians held a common view of religion. The Supreme God or Great Manitou ruled from the sky for the good of all. Lesser but important sky manitous were the Sun, Moon, Stars, the Four Winds, the Thunderbird (with its thunder and lightning), and the earth, which the Central Algonquians knew as Grandmother. All these manitous bestowed their kindnesses and benefits upon the tribespeople. Unfortunately, there were also evil manitous who were dedicated to making life miserable. These malevolent ghosts and monsters lurked under the earth.

This vast spiritual world included just about everything in nature~animals, birds, trees, rocks, and in fact everything above or below the earth and its waters. All had spirits that must be respected. Every tribesperson, in childhood or at least by puberty, would seek his or her own spirit guardian through visions and dreams. In times of need this unseen force could be called upon for help, guidance, and protection. These vision quests were almost unknown among the southeastern tribes.

Four steps were taken to call upon a supernatural protector or to contact the even greater manitous. The Algonquian's face was blackened to gain the attention of the Fire spirit, who was the messenger to the spirit world. Fasting cleansed his or her inner being and encouraged communication through dreams or visions. Wailing and moaning hopefully brought pity and help from the manitou. Above all, it was hoped the smoke of the sacred tobacco, sent skyward, would attract notice as an offering. Because supernatural beings craved tobacco more than anything else, it was prudent to give a present of tobacco leaves. Since the leaf was grown only by humans the manitou would be both pleased and obligated to use the spirit of the tobacco.

The power received from the unseen guardians was represented by objects that had been seen in the vision quest. They might include a palm drill for making a sacred ceremonial fire, medicinal herbs, rounded stone "thunder eggs" (i.e., rounded stones), roots, powders, fetishes, miniature weapons and lacross sticks, and pictographs on leather or birch bark. These mystical objects were held in a sacred bundle~often a decorated skin bag of otter or mink~for safe-keeping. Bundles would be passed down through later generations. Each Sky and Earth division would have its own major bundle, deserving of twice-a-year ceremonials with feasting, dancing, songs, and a recounting of the original vision quest at the beginnings of the division and its subsequent history. In doing so, both manitou and keepers of the sacred bundles would be reminded of their obligations.

PALM RESTS FOR TOP OF THE BOW DRILL

Like the southeastern Indians, the Algonquian tribes considered their medicine men or shamans to be intermediaries between the spirit world and the patient. His powers were formidable, for he could not only heal but could inflict illness. His service was for a fee, and the larger the payment, the surer the cure. In most cases a wicked spirit had taken over the patient's soul, and it must be coaxed or sucked into the shaman's bone tube. The treatment would be accompanied by a rattle and the appropriate incantations, and sometimes ventriloquism, juggling, and magic tricks. The medicine man's other services might include medicine for a successful hunt and powders and charms that would make the buyer irresistible to the opposite sex.

The Medicine Lodge Society was the oldest and best known of the Algonquian medical organizations. Its rituals were guarantees of good health and a long life~probably beginning after payment. Each member had his own medicine bag of curative powders and usually a cowrie shell that could be "shot" (mystically propelled) into the patient along with the medicines that could remove the shell along with the illness. Since sickness could be due to a disregard for the manitou or to not thanking the spirits for a successful hunt or other good fortune, the practitioner might appease them by ritualistic offerings. The variations in any shamanistic practice, however, were infinite.

WINNEBAGO SACRED BUNDLE OF A WHOLE OTTER PELT

GAMES AND CELEBRATIONS

Holidays and games were a welcome change from the daily demands for food, clothing and shelter. One of the better southeastern traditions that caught on in the rest of the woodlands was lacrosse. Competition among the Central Algonquians' peace and war divisions was every bit as fierce and bruising as the lacrosse played today. The game was designed to develop the competitive spirit, strength, and agility of the young tribal warriors. It has been said that as many as a thousand braves in full war paint would compete on the field. The ball was carried or thrown in a "cross" ~ a hickory-framed racquet with a rawhide or gut-laced netting, not unlike a modern baseball player's glove. The ball was scooped up and thrown at the goal net. It could be kicked, but no hand could touch it except for the goalkeeper, who batted it with his hand.

The women played a less brutal game with a straight stick and a double ball. There were also contests of archery, wrestling, and snowsnake. Whatever the game, gambling would be its constant companion. This Indian addiction needn't wait for the large tribal contests. An everyday gambling favorite was the moccasin game. One of four small objects, such as a pebble, was marked in an inconspicuous way. Each was placed in a separate moccasin and guesses were made as to which held the marked object. After a game, it was not uncommon for a loser to be left with nothing more than a breechclout to his name. Not to be outdone, the women gambled with bone dice that were rolled from a wooden container.

WARFARE

The games were training grounds for war, which a young man might experience when he approached his sixteenth birthday. By then, most of the girls his age would have married. But when the war chief called his council together by sending each member a red-stained wampum belt, the would-be warrior might soon be on his first warpath. Upon agreement of the chief and his council, the war party was organized. The night before the attack, the sacred bundles of the Earth division were combined and carried at the front of the column by the war chief or shaman. Upon returning, the bundles were carried behind the party. They were always kept between the attackers and their enemy. An all-night war dance preceded the attack, and the young brave would be among the numbers there, ready to prove his bravery ~ if, and only if, he chose to join them. (See pages 81-83 for similar attack strategies of the Coastal Algonquians.)

Generally the raids were not large. After a surprise attack, members would be retracing their steps ~ but

CONTESTANTS LAUNCHED WAXED WOODEN SNOWSNAKES FOR DISTANCE DOWN A LENGTHY SNOW TROUGH.

not before dispatching to eternity any of the young, elderly, and infirm males. They might delay the victorious return march and would surely provide enviable scalp trophies. Women were brought back for possible tribal adoption. Warrior prisoners might also have the happy fate of being adopted by village widows if they could run the gauntlet and if they proved themselves on later war parties. Any other warrior prisoners must prepare themselves for torture.

THE SEASONAL ROUNDS

The seasonal rounds for the Central (as well as the Coastal) Algonquians began when spring breathed new life into the earth—or didn't. Within ten to twenty years, after all, cultivated soils at an existing village would become overworked and nonproductive. It would then be time to select and ready a new village site and surrounding garden plots for the coming year. To start, the men leveled trees by burning the bases and then gradually chipping away the char with their stone axes, gouges, and celts. The women could break up the sods and discourage any seedlings that would replace the felled trees.

GARDENING, FISHING, AND PRESERVING

The planting season began when the white oak leaves were as large as a mouse's ears. (The garden plots and their crops were owned by the individual households.) Women began by mounding the soil between stumps every 3 feet or so. With a sharpened stick, four holes for the four compass directions were punched into the soil for the corn seed. Later, pole beans would be added to the mounds, to make use of the corn stalk as a support for the climbing bean vines. Squash, pumpkins, sunflowers, and gourds for natural containers were set apart from the mounds so that they would not be shaded by the cornstalks. Tobacco was in its own separate plot and was the only crop managed by the men. They would later add willow to make their Kinnikinnick tobacco or mix the crushed leaves and roots of the dwarf sumac for tobacco for ceremonial use. Probably the latter would be used in the Green Corn Dance for the first fruit harvest as a "thank you" to the benevolent spirits.

The spring spawning runs brought most of the men to their temporary riverside camps. The Central Algonquians caught fish all along the inland waterways by suspending nets with floats and plummet weights, using net scoops on poles, spearing or shooting fish with bows and arrows in the shallows, or spearing them from canoes at night aided by the light of a flaming chunk of bark wedged on a pole. Weirs and fish traps let the current of a stream do the work.

As summer blended into fall, the women and children continued their gathering of berries, roots, nuts, and such seasonal greens as dandelion, watercress, and mustard to boil with the meat. The first

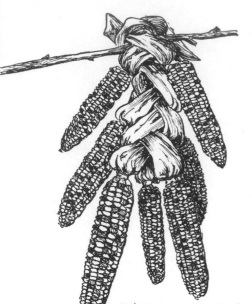

THE STRIPPED HUSKS WERE BRAIDED AND THE EARS HUNG UP TO DRY.

DRIED CORN KERNELS COULD BE SCRAPED FROM THE COBS WITH A MANDIBLE FROM A DEER.

corn harvest and the Green Corn ceremonials had passed. It had been widely celebrated throughout the woodlands and would be one of the few holidays celebrated among the more scattered Algonquians. There was still the sweet corn stalk pith for the youngsters to suck or make into toys like mini-ducks and dolls.

Their mothers were busy grinding the dried corn for corn mush, flavored with berries, nuts, or maple sugar. Bread dough was made from corn flour and water and was then wrapped in husks and baked in embers. Stew simmered in a cone-shaped or round-bottomed pot set into the hearth and surrounded by fire. Meat, fish, beans, squash, nuts, greens ~ whatever was on hand ~ went into the pot to give a variety of different flavors. Bones and other inedibles just settled to the bottom of the pot. While mealtimes were determined by hunger and convenience, the Algonquians generally collected the family for morning and evening dining. Their eating utensils would include shells, gourds, bark, and carved wooden containers that served as spoons, ladles, dishes, and bowls.

With winter just down the path, food preservation continued. Women shelled the dried corn ears and stored them in woven bags in corn cribs and mat- and bark-lined storage pits. (The Pilgrims warded off starvation when they discovered Indian "barns" at their first Cape Cod landing.) Beans were sun-dried and squash, cut into rings, might be smoked.

The Central Algonquian Chippewa and Ojibwa tribes of Wisconsin and Minnesota laid in winter stores of wild rice (*Zizania aquatica* ~ no relation to our modern cooking rice). While the men poled their canoes through the extensive grain-and-water flats, the women, who were seated inside, lowered bunches of stalks into the canoe and knocked off the grains with a pair of cedar sticks. After the Algonquians dried the rice over the hearth, they removed the husks by spreading the grain on a sheet of leather and crushing them underfoot. Then they winnowed the chaff by repeatedly tossing the rice in a birch bark tray. The grains had a long preservation life in the cold months ahead.

In late autumn, after the leaves had fallen, and sometimes in the spring, the forest brush and brambles were cleared with controlled fires. The bark armor of the great trees preserved them and gave the forest a parklike appearance. Tracking and travel were made considerably easier.

By the time cold weather had come, the women had stripped off the mat or bark sheathing that covered their village wigwams. Once these were rolled up and backpacked into more protected winter quarters, the women could use them to shingle the frameworks made by the men. Once the family was snug enough, the men were off on their winter hunts. Not only would they bring back a fresh quantity of meat, but also pelts, which were at their best in the cold months.

From Delaware westward to Missouri the warmer days and chilly nights of late winter brought on a flow of sap. Sugar maple and birch trees ~ and sometimes soft maple, box elder, and hickory ~ were tapped by cutting a slanted or V-shaped gash in the bark. A pithy twig, such as elderberry, was inserted at the lowest point of the cut, and a bark container below it caught the sweet drippings. The ice from an overnight freeze could be skimmed off for a more concentrated sap, or the whole could be boiled to a syrup, or, with more cooking time, to the crystallized maple sugar. Eight pounds of boiled sap yielded one pound of sugar for flavoring or a candy treat.

SUGAR MAPLE

HUNTING

The business of hunting was not taken lightly. Each animal had a spirit that must be appeased if the hunt was to be successful. Prayer and tobacco sacrifices must be offered at the outset. Deer might be decoyed within arrow range by the hunter, who wore an antlered deer head. Deer, bear, moose, and lesser animals ~ turkey, partridge, and quail ~ were tracked and taken by arrow, snares, and deadfalls. Passenger pigeons were so plentiful that they sometimes darkened the sky, and south-bound flyways gave up their share of ducks and geese. When the snows came, the tracking of moose, deer, and caribou through the drifts was made a great deal easier with a pair of snowshoes.

There were other hunting aids that made a full kettle back home more certain. Deer calls of cedar bark and moose calls of birch bark might attract an inquisitive target. Dogs had been valued companions ever since the first Paleo-Americans crossed the Bering Strait with these four-legged tracking experts. Although the Late Woodland creatures had sharp, foxlike heads, wolflike bodies, and howled instead of barked, they were indeed true dogs. They were well trained and could flush out a game bird or retrieve it from the water.

There were spring deer drives during which the entire village turned out. Men, women, and children formed a

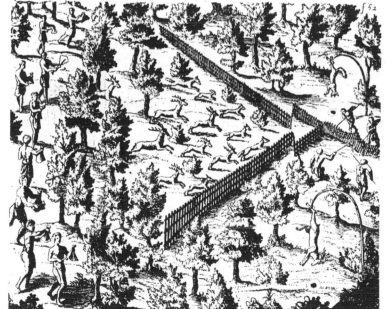

A HURON DEER DRIVE AS ILLUSTRATED IN SAMUEL DE CHAMPLAIN'S VOYAGES PARIS, 1619

63

great arc in the woods. Making all the racket they could, the villagers moved toward a funnel-shaped fence, driving the game before them. Hunters' arrows were ready where the fencing narrowed. Or the deer might be driven onto a peninsula and taken by canoe when they attempted to swim to safety.

STAGES OF LIFE

INFANCY AND CHILDHOOD

Central Algonquian women were isolated in a small lodge when ready to give birth. An experienced midwife might be on hand for a more difficult delivery. The mother and child remained separated from the rest of the village for ten or more days. The infant would be given a name, often one from the husband's clan lineage, providing no living clansmember possessed it. Among the Chippewa and probably other Central Algonquian tribes, a cradleboard would be the infant's bed for the first year. It and its contents could be hung on a limb while the mother worked or carried on her back, secured to a tumpline around her forehead. Sphagnum moss, cattail or milkweed fluff, or duck feathers provided a comfortable and absorbent mattress. The decorated restraint bindings would be removed regularly for cleaning and to allow the infant some exercise. The infant's moccasins had precautionary holes in the soles in case the evil spirits attempted to kidnap him or her to the world of the dead. With this foot gear, the infant couldn't undertake such a journey.

THE WOODEN CRADLE-BOARD FRAME WOULD BE PADDED BEFORE THE INFANT WAS STRAPPED INTO IT. THE BOWED STRIP SUPPORTED A DEERSKIN ROOFING TO KEEP THE HEAD SHADED.

Most youngsters didn't wear a stitch of clothing during the warm summer months until the age of six. By then the boys had become decent shots, taking small critters with their bows and arrows. Girls learned such chores as planting, cooking, and weaving from their mother. Children were rarely disciplined except for lectures on their shortcomings. There were times, however, when a child was punished by enforced fasting, switching, or a dunk in cold water. All in all, there was never a lack of praise and encouragement. For example, after an Illinois boy had killed his first game, the event was celebrated with a ritual feast, songs and prayers. It was a happy-go-lucky time of life with few worries or

64

responsibilities.

PUBERTY

Puberty — that giant step between childhood and becoming an adult — was marked by the all-important vision quest. In the isolation of the deep woods a young man would fast for up to ten days in preparation for his dream vision. His guardian spirit, usually in the form of an animal, would reveal itself and give its new ward the benefit of its supernatural powers. Through the dream vision the young man would understand his spiritual obligations in the feasts, dances, games, and songs that were held throughout the year. He could call on his unseen guardian for strength, encouragement, and direction in his adult life. A Menominee boy would have his dream encounter interpreted by a shaman.

A girl, at her first menstrual period, would seclude herself in the same lodge that was used during childbirth. There she would fast until her unseen guardian would make a dream visitation and give her directions for her religious duties as an adult. In some tribes, such as the Fox, both sexes painted their faces red to show their adult status. Promiscuity among teenagers was common.

ADULTHOOD AND THE
BONDS OF MATRIMONY

Prospective husbands in the Miami, Fox, and Kickapoo tribes started courtship on a romantic note. In the dark of night, the young man entered the young woman's lodge with a birch-bark torch. If she smiled when she asked him to leave, she accepted the proposal and he might stay the night. The parents may have arranged the meeting, but in any event must approve of the coming marriage. An exchange of gifts gave their consent.

In contrast, an Illinois young man could not accept the responsibility of marriage until he had proved himself on the hunt and on several war parties. Chippewa mothers and grandmothers kept close watch on their maidens. The couple could visit only under their watchful eyes. Marriage was then arranged by the man's family. Monogamy was the rule, although men of importance might have two and rarely three wives. Divorce among the Chippewa and other Central Algonquian tribes was simple enough. All the woman need do was to return to the lodge of her parents. Simple, but not easily done, for divorce reflected upon the judgment of the parents, who gave their approval for marriage.

A GOOD PROVIDER WAS WELL ON THE TRAIL TO MARRIAGE.

65

OLD AGE AND DEATH

Those tribespeople who had reached old age were cared for and were highly respected. Their spiritual powers had grown through the years, and they were well prepared for the world beyond. In death, the body was dressed in finery by members of the opposite moiety, or tribal division. The Illinois painted the hair and face red, were generous with their grave goods, and reenacted the person's favorite activities, such as games, gambling, and dancing, during the burial ceremonies. The Chippewa dead were laid in a westerly direction and were told by the shaman the best trail to take and the dangers awaiting them on their journey to the sky village. Shawnee souls were asked not to look back or think of those who must remain on earth. Generally, a surviving spouse mourned for a year without paint or jewelry before marrying.

During the past few centuries, the Central Algonquians' world was turned upside down. The might of the Iroquois fell upon them early in the seventeenth century, and by midcentury the Sauks, Kickapoos, Foxes, and the Potowatomis were dispersed into the Wisconsin lands of the Menominis and Winnebagos. The Shawnees and the Miamis were also displaced as the French fur traders pushed into their tribal lands. The Ojibwas fled to Minnesota and in turn drove out the Eastern Dakotas. Tribal identity blurred in the massive shuffle. By the early nineteenth century, the remnants of these once powerful Central Algonquians again fled westward ~ this time across the Mississippi River ~ before the expanding United States' settlements. It is regrettable that their history has been so badly fragmented.

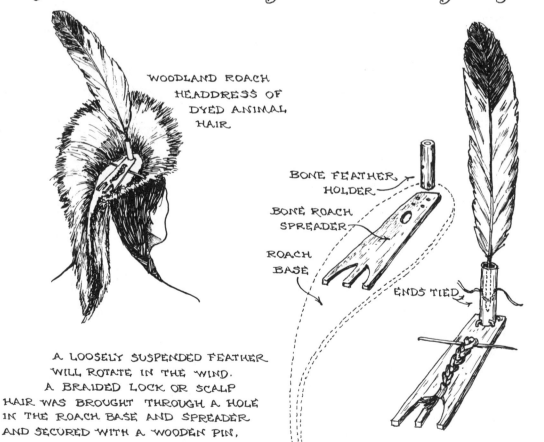

WOODLAND ROACH HEADDRESS OF DYED ANIMAL HAIR

BONE FEATHER HOLDER

BONE ROACH SPREADER

ROACH BASE

ENDS TIED

A LOOSELY SUSPENDED FEATHER WILL ROTATE IN THE WIND. A BRAIDED LOCK OR SCALP HAIR WAS BROUGHT THROUGH A HOLE IN THE ROACH BASE AND SPREADER AND SECURED WITH A WOODEN PIN.

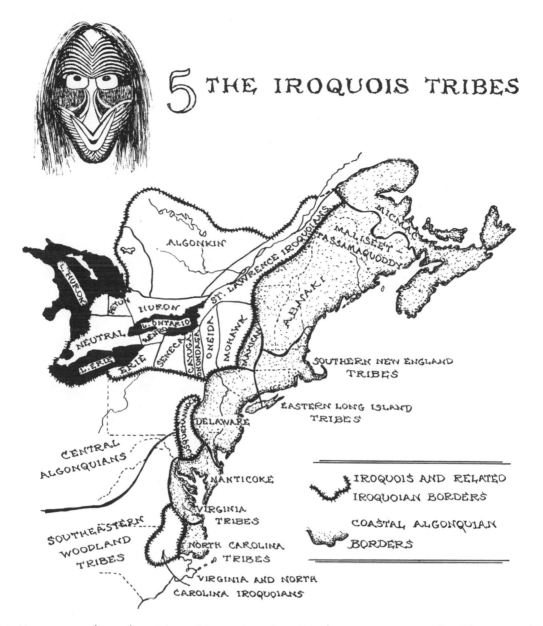

5 THE IROQUOIS TRIBES

Well up and into the New York State region of the northeastern woodlands were the pre-Iroquois people. Between A.D. 1000 and 1300 the Hopewell-influenced Point Peninsula Phase had developed into the Owasco Phase, with the Iroquoian language solidly in place. (See the Early Woodland Period, page 33.) Its inspiration was the Mississippian emphasis on cultivated gardens and those crops that could be grown in colder latitudes. One of the oldest varieties was the Flour, or soft, corn that could be easily ground when dried. Northern Flint corn matured in a relatively few weeks and Sweet corn was ideal for roasting and eating on the cob. By A.D. 1100 beans, squash, pumpkins, and sunflowers for seeds were feeding hungry Iroquoians. Tobacco had become an important part of their religious rituals. Traditional hunting and fishing were now running second best to cultivation among the Iroquois.

Gardening by the women in the small and scattered family bands was so successful that the pre-Iroquois gathered into hamlets, where they could be surrounded by acres of prime fields for cultivation. Hamlets grew into villages, where families joined

67

other relatives to build the large, clan-oriented long-houses. In the matrilineal Iroquoian society of common female ancestors, a man married into a clan other than his own and joined his wife in her extended family longhouse. In this women's world, the dwelling and furnishings, the village or town itself, and the cleared and planted fields beyond were their domain. It was the senior clan women who chose their next male chieftain from the same matrilineage as his predecessor. If that clan representative fell short of expectations, he could be removed by the elder females.

TOBACCO ~ MAN'S SACRED CROP

CONDUCTING AND CONTAINING HOSTILITIES

Except for the clan chieftains, who met with the village elders and wise men of the village council, the role of the Owasco-Iroquois men was changing from hunter-provider to protector-avenger. The village must be stockaded and the garden fields protected from raiders from other villages. Clan loyalty was fierce and uncompromising when it came to avenging a wrong inflicted on one of its members by another village or town. These blood feuds erupted into a range of hostilities, from small-scale raids and ambushes conducted by clan braves acting on their own to all-out intervillage warfare with council sanction. The brave and daring warrior was glorified when the took an enemy scalp or head as a trophy or brought back his own prisoner. Women and children captives would either be marched back to the victor's village to replace those massacred from enemy attack or would be dispatched on the spot with a war club. By the seventeenth century Jesuit observers noted that the Iroquois population had been so badly decimated by war that the captives outnumbered the villagers.

CLAN BLOOD REVENGE

A captive warrior could expect one of several fates. He would be bound with special prisoner ties and displayed on a raised platform in the victorious village for all to see. His one slim hope for survival depended upon a village widow choosing him as a replacement for her fallen husband ~ provided that he could successfully run the gauntlet. Two long lines of villagers, armed with sticks and clubs, did their best to knock their sprinting target to the ground. He who was still on his feet at the end of the obstacle course was rewarded with his life, a new name, and a chance to prove his loyalty to a village he previously despised. Failure, however, meant certain torture and death.

This treatment of prisoners was shared by the other Late Woodland peoples, although to a lesser extent. What set these Owasco-Iroquois apart was their fascination for the Mississippian southeastern sacrificial traditions. First came the torture. The prisoner's fingernails might be pulled out, and the fingers he would use to draw back a bowstring were chopped off. Similar mutilations might continue for five to six days, during which time he would be lectured on the wrong his people had inflicted. He in turn would mock his captors and sing his own war song before his last energy and life itself ebbed away. He had been sacrificed to the God of War. If he had faced death undaunted, his heart would be removed and ritually eaten by the young warriors to give them his courage. There followed the ceremonial roasting and eating of his flesh.

AN IROQUOIS WARRIOR TORCHING A PRISONER, AFTER A SKETCH BY SEVENTEENTH CENTURY DUTCH VISITOR DAVID DE VRIES

THE GREAT CONFEDERACY

As the Owasco-Iroquoian Phase came to an end around A.D 1300, wiser heads were devising better ways to end the escalating blood feuds. Legend had it that divine inspiration came from the Great Spirit Deganawidah, who had been born of a virgin mother. He was aided by the noble Mohawk chieftain Hiawatha in bringing peace to the villages of the five developing Iroquois tribes. It was declared that all Iroquois were created equal and a part of one great brotherhood. All could make council together to settle common differences and concerns in one great League of the Iroquois. (The formal name was Confederacy of the Iroquois, but the Iroquois themselves called it the People of the Longhouse. Historians usually refer to it as the League of the Iroquois.) Many believe that the federal plan of the United States was modeled after this alliance

By A.D. 1600 the league could provide a democratic forum for the Mohawk, Oneida, Onondaga, Cayuga, and Seneca tribes. Its fifty voting representatives were made up in part of the matrilineal village chieftains of each tribe. Other league council

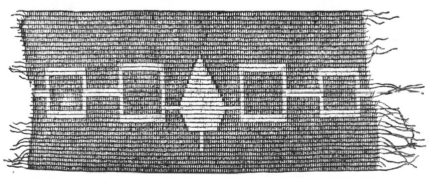

ONONDAGA WAMPUM BELT SAID TO REPRESENT THE FORMATION OF THE IROQUOIAN LEAGUE ~ "ONE HEART FOR ALL THE NATIONS"

members were the Pine Tree Chiefs ~ leaders who had distinguished themselves as warriors and had risen in the ranks through merit rather than by clan inheritance. Although they had no voting rights, they could speak their minds to counterbalance the opinions of the tribal chiefs. It was up to the league chieftains to approve or reject the Pine Tree Chiefs' views. Their fundamental goal was to put an end to the clan blood feuds and the intertribal wars. Problems within a tribal village remained for the village chief and his council to solve. When the Tuscarora Iroquoians fled northward from North Carolina in 1723 (see page 74), they were formally accepted as the sixth member of the League of the Iroquois.

WARFARE

Although the Iroquoian taste for war no longer pitted brother against brother, the warrior's glory path against Algonquian neighbors remained open and inviting. It was for good reason that the nearby Narragansett tribe called the Mohawks "mohowaugsuck" or man-eaters. And when an all-out war against the French and their Huron allies was approved by the League of the Iroquois, for example, their collective might erased the Hurons from the face of the earth. As we shall see, Iroquoian aggression grew and spread in all directions of the compass during the Early Historic Period. Between offensives, the young hotbloods could take out their hostilities in competitive games and ceremonial dances. All but the Mohawks and Oneidas had moieties within each clan.

THE SPIRIT WORLD

While the Mohawk, Oneida, Onondaga, Cayuga, and Seneca tribes are remembered for their peace among themselves and war against outsiders, their people were not all that different from the Central

IROQUOIS MAPLE
BALL-HEADED CLUB

PRISONER HALTER, CAUGHNAWAGA, MOHAWK, QUEBEC
THE COLLAR WAS WRAPPED AROUND THE NECK OF A PRISONER, WHO WAS LED AWAY BY TWO VICTORS, ONE IN FRONT, ONE BEHIND. THE INSIDE OF THE COLLAR WAS FILLED WITH SHARP HEDGEHOG QUILLS. THIS ONE WAS TAKEN IN A RAID ON DEERFIELD, MASSACHUSETTS IN 1746.
MEMORIAL HALL, OLD DEERFIELD, MASSACHUSETTS

and Coastal Algonquians around them. They shared similar beliefs in supernatural powers, with their own slant on creation. It was said that the Sky Woman fell from the heavens and was saved by the efforts of the animals diving into the waters. They scooped up quantities of soft mud and covered the mythical Turtle's back for her safe landing. She gave birth to a daughter, who in turn bore the Twin Brothers. One was the Great Spirit, who created such beneficial spiritual beings as the Sun God (who controlled hunting and warfare), Rain and Thunder Gods, the wind spirits, and the congenial and beautiful Three Sisters, who represented corn, squash, and beans. The other Twin Brother was understandably known as the Evil Spirit. He was dedicated to the heaping of misery upon the people through the creation of monsters, witches, demons, ghosts of the dead, poisonous snakes and plants, and fearsome natural calamities. Countless other unseen spirits, both good and bad, were everywhere, practicing their helpfulness or mischief.

FALSE-FACE
SOCIETY MASK

The False Face Society represented the mask spirit, who protected humans from disease and illness in addition to giving encouragement to the winds and acting as a gamekeeper. The Society's members wore grotesque wooden masks carved from a living basswood tree. The masks represented beings of the forest or the dream world. When worn, they gave the wearer special healing powers. Twice yearly, members visited the longhouses to clear out disease. Another mask-wearing organization was the Husk Face Society. When wearing these woven and braided corn husk faces, members could communicate with the horticultural spirit world — an important effort, considering the Iroquoian dependence on their cultivated crops. Most of the masking ceremonies probably date to the Owasco period, and there were many other societies that focused on assorted spirits and deities through dances, songs, and costumed rituals.

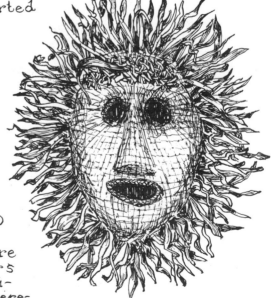

HUSK FACE SOCIETY MASK

CRAFTS OF
THE IROQUOIS

Clay was the ideal medium to express one's creativity, and Iroquoian pottery had an individuality all its own. During the Owasco period, between A.D. 1000 and 1300, the women made many round-bottomed pots with distinctive collars that were often castellated. Only the necks and collars were decorated with geometric designs, incisions, or cord-wrapped paddle embossings. Thereafter and up to the Contact Period, the collars

71

OWASCO POT WITH CORD-
WRAPPED-STICK IMPRESSIONS
ON COLLAR, NECK, AND BODY
~ CASTLE CREEK SITE ~

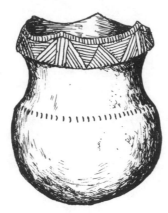

LATE MOHAWK-ONEIDA-ONONDAGA
~ FONDA INCISED ~

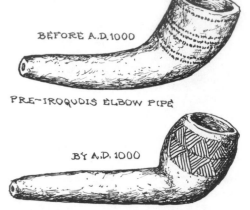

BEFORE A.D. 1000

PRE-IROQUOIS ELBOW PIPE

BY A.D. 1000

OWASCO ELBOW PIPE WITH BARREL BOWL

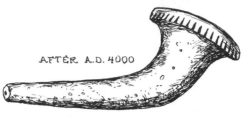

AFTER A.D. 4000

IROQUOIS TRUMPET PIPE

bore incised markings that were oblique,
V-shaped, or horizontal. Since the cultivation of the sacred tobacco was the province
of men, it wasn't surprising that they also
crafted their ceremonial clay pipes. The earlier elbow pipes had had
barrel-shaped bowls during the Owasco period. By A.D. 1400 the unique
trumpet pipes came into fashion and were sometimes embellished with
animal or human effigies. Since over 90 percent of the Iroquoian
artifacts found are ceramics, their changing styles are important clues
for dating and the identity of their makers ~ as they are in the rest
of the woodlands.

The Iroquois were distinguished by their concentration in larger
towns to better service their crops; their highly organized tribal politics;
ability to form outstanding confederacies, such as the League of the Iroquois;
and their aggressiveness and glorification of war and prisoner sacrifice.
In other ways, the Iroquois people were fairly typical of the northeastern
woodland tribes. Although their villages were of a more permanent nature,
they made their seasonal rounds like the Central Algonquians and others.
(See page 60.) They reached adulthood in much the same way (see
Stages of Life, page 64). And at death, the opposite moiety buried
them in the flexed position with a few grave goods. A Feast of the
Dead would follow a period of mourning, and at that time the soul
made its way to the spirit world in the west.

OTHER IROQUOIS-SPEAKING TRIBES

A number of related tribes were clustered around the core of
Five Nation Iroquois in New York. All were branch-offs from the
Owasco period, and all were Iroquoian speakers with similar traditions.
The ancestors of the Cherokee were clustered in villages around Lakes
Erie and Ontario before their migration southward between A.D. 1000
and 2000. On the northern shores were the Neutrals, so dubbed by
the French because they took no sides while sandwiched between
the Iroquois and the Hurons. Further east were the St. Lawrence

THE COASTAL ALGONQUIANS

🐛 COASTAL ALGONQUIANS
🐛 IROQUOIS - IROQUOIANS

MICMAC

MALISEET

ST. LAWRENCE IROQUOIS

EASTERN ABENAKI

PASSAMAQUODDY

WESTERN ABENAKI

MERRIMAC RIVER

IROQUOIS

MAHICAN

ERIE

WENRO

SOUTHERN NEW ENGLAND ALGONQUIANS

LONG ISLAND

CENTRAL ALGONQUIANS

SUSQUEHANNOCK

DELAWARE

POTOMAC R.

NANTICOKE

VIRGINIAN ALGONQUIANS

SOUTHERN IROQUOIS

SOUTHEASTERN TRIBES

NORTH CAROLINA ALGONQUIANS

Iroquois, who were visited by Jacques Cartier in 1535. Southward along the North Branch of the Susquehanna River was the Susquehannock tribe, and still further south, the Nottoway and Tuscarora Iroquoians had infiltrated into the foothills of North Carolina and Virginia, becoming unwelcome neighbors to the southeastern Coastal Algonquians.

They had everything but friendship in common. Once the bloody clan revenges among the five Iroquois tribes ended with their League of the Iroquois confederacy, their war-oriented braves turned their fury on the other Iroquoian speakers.

When the Hurons monopolized the fur trade with the French, a thousand Mohawk and Seneca warriors exploded on them in 1649. The annihilation was so complete that the Hurons no longer existed as a tribe. Within six short years, the rampaging Five Nations crushed the Tobacco Nation, the Eries, the Neutrals, and the Susquehannas.

The Susquehannocks were staggered, perhaps, but not to be counted out. The remnants moved to the more distant and safer Lancaster County in Pennsylvania, gained strength, and turned on their Coastal Algonquian neighbors, the Delawares. Meanwhile, the fur trade with the colonists had resulted in intense intertribal competition for new hunting lands. In these Beaver Wars, the Maryland-backed Susquehannocks invaded their old enemies, the Seneca and Cayuga Iroquois. There they soundly thrashed the western Iroquois.

As fate would have it, an unseen enemy, smallpox, swept through the Susquehannock people. As was mentioned earlier, in the isolation of the American continent, they and all other Indian tribes had no immunity to the Old World diseases. By the mid-1670s, the Iroquois nations took over the Susquehannock lands from the survivors with-

THIS SUSQUEHANNOCK WARRIOR APPEARED ON CAPTAIN JOHN SMITH'S MAP OF 1612.

out even a single major battle. The Iroquois were now masters of the Northeast, free to extract tributes of their choosing from the Algonquian tribes. As the ever-increasing numbers of French traders and English colonists came into conflict, the League of the Iroquois were in the enviable position of holding the balance of power between the opposing forces They remained a power until the American Revolution split the League and the westward expansion of settlers overwhelmed its members.

Farther south and widely separated from their Five Nations kin were the Iroquoian-speaking Tuscarora tribe of North Carolina and the Nottoway and Meherrin tribes of Virginia. They had infiltrated into the foothills of the southern Algonquian lands by A.D. 500. In another five hundred years they had elbowed their way into the greater part of the Algonquians' North Carolina. As with the other Iroquoian speakers, they were well organized in tribal politics and the ways of war. They wintered in the traditional straight-sided, dome-topped, mat- or bark-covered longhouses, which were well stockaded. In the summertime and when hunting, they lived in the more temporary dome-shaped wigwams that were more characteristic of the Algonquians.

The Tuscaroras ultimately were beset by unscrupulous, land-grabbing colonists, then defeated in a series of uprisings. They took the long trek northward to the lands of their origin and became the sixth nation in the League of Iroquois in 1722. The fate of the Nottoway and Meherrin rested with the neighboring Algonquian tribes, as will be noted shortly.

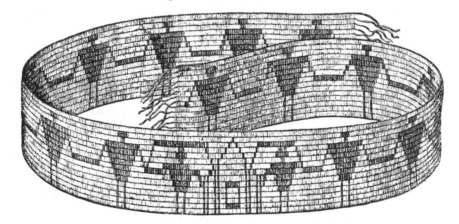

THIS HANDSOME ONONDAGA WAMPUM BELT MAY
REPRESENT THE BEGINNINGS OF THE LEAGUE OF THE IROQUOIS.

74

THE COASTAL ALGONQUIAN TRIBES

The Atlantic Ocean and the Appalachian Mountain chain were the natural barriers that had kept the Coastal Algonquians intact. From North Carolina on up to the far reaches of Nova Scotia, they had continued the simpler lifestyle of their Archaic forefathers. Despite regional dialects, their common tongue permitted a diffusion of ideas and customs all along the coastline. Any tribal differences revolved around their regional climate, natural resources, and influences from the infiltration of other tribes.

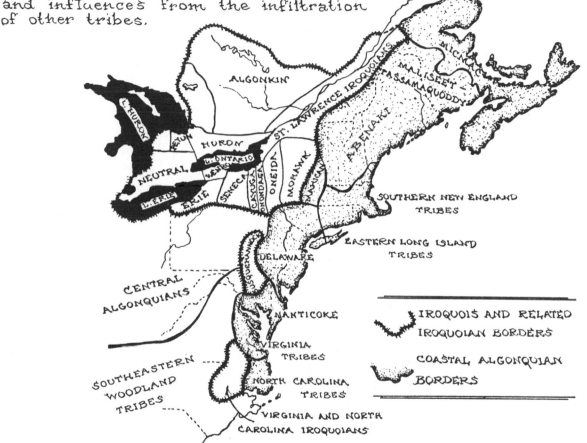

The Appalachian foothills were blessed with a warmth that produced plentiful harvests on the flat, coastal plains and an extended season for fishing and gathering shellfish along the waterways. The Coastal Algonquian summer wigwams dotted the shore, where the families could gather shellfish. Their great shell middens stand as monuments to their love of this seafood. Quahogs could be gathered only as far north as Maine and oysters up to Cape Breton Island, but the hardy softshell clam made it all the way to Greenland. Like the fish catches, the shellfish were dried over smoky fires that also kept pesky insects away. With less need to shift with the seasons, the southern villages could be more permanent.

The midcoastal tribes, who lived between the Potomac River and

New England's Merrimack River, also depended on crops and seafood. The spring spawning runs brought most of the men to their temporary riverside camps. In New England, the shad and herring runs netted such quantities that they were used as garden fertilizer ~ these woodlanders were probably the only ones to enrich their soil that way. The Coastal Algonquians caught fish all along the seashores, its estuaries, and (like the Central Algonquians) the inland waterways by using nets with floats and weights, nets on poles, spears, and bows and arrows.

But with winter's chill came the need to move to the protected upriver forests for hunting and gathering of fall roots and nuts. Brief summers and lengthy snows above the Merrimack allowed for few if any gardens during the summer fishing and shellfishing season. Then they must beat a retreat to their inland winter hunting camps with their wigwam coverings to sheath the still-standing frameworks.

The coastal isolation was far from complete. The Early Woodland Adena-Hopewell traders had impressed the Algonquians with their handsome grave goods, even though the grave-mound culture itself had been shrugged off. Then there were the aggressive Iroquoian speakers who had expanded their control all along the western bounds of the Algonquian lands. It was inevitable that the central tribes absorb some of the Iroquoian arts and beliefs. But the most profound influences would come from the east. What began as a trickle of European traders and fishermen in the sixteenth century soon became a tidal wave of settlers with trade goods that no Stone Ager could resist. Tribal lands and tribal culture were up for grabs.

MAJOR SOUTHERN NEW ENGLAND TRIBES

THE VILLAGES

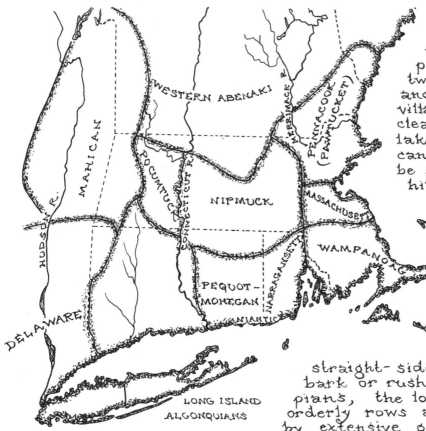

LONG ISLAND ALGONQUIANS

Generally speaking, the Algonquian villages along the coast were small ~ perhaps averaging but ten to twelve dwellings ~ scattered, and self-sufficient. An ideal village site would have its crystal-clear running spring and a river, lake, or seashore for fishing and canoe travel. Perhaps it would be stockaded on the crest of a hill for better defense, with mountains or elevated forests to the north to ward off wintry winds.

In the southeast the dwellings were permanent, scaled-down longhouses between 25 and 50 feet in length that held up to twenty family members. In the Iroquois tradition, they were straight-sided and dome-capped with bark or rush sheathing. Like the Mississippians, the longhouses were arranged in orderly rows around a plaza, surrounded by extensive gardens. The midcoastal villages had similar clan longhouses, but they

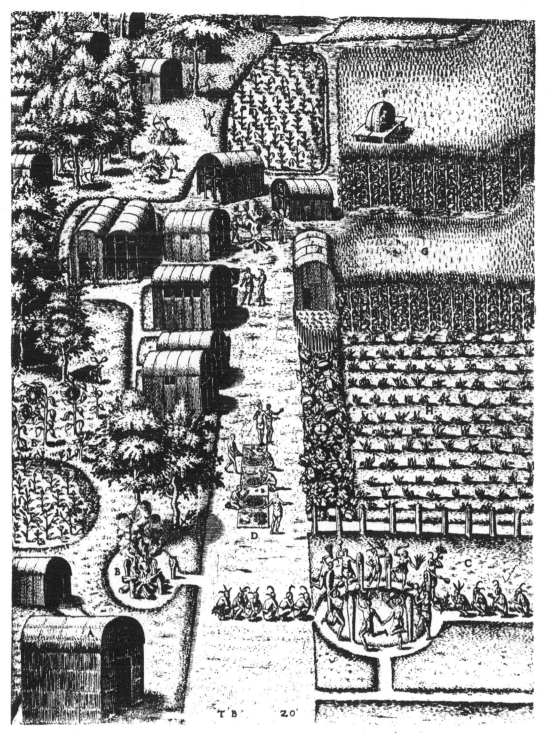

THE COASTAL NORTH CAROLINA VILLAGE OF SECOTAN

THIS DE BRY ENGRAVING OF JOHN WHITE'S WATERCOLOR FIRST APPEARED IN THE 1590 EDITION OF THOMAS HARIOT'S BRIEFE AND TRUE REPORT OF THE NEW FOUND LAND OF VIRGINIA.

A. BUILDING HOLDING TOMBS OF CHIEFTAINS
B. A PLACE FOR PRAYER
C. AREA FOR FEASTING AND CELEBRATIONS
D. PLACE WHERE THEY MAKE MERRY AFTER C.
E. SEPARATE GARDEN FOR SACRED TOBACCO
F. WATCHMAN MAKES CONSTANT NOISE TO SCARE

AWAY BIRDS AND ANIMALS IN CORNFIELD
G. CORN FIELD
H. CORN PLANTED SEPARATELY
I. PUMPKIN GARDEN
K. SITE FOR FEAST FIRES
L. RIVER SUPPLIES THE VILLAGE WATER

were widely separated in no particular pattern to allow for neighboring garden plots. If the village was stockaded, the houses would necessarily be more bunched together.

In southern New England, there were also village longhouses of a different profile. Instead of vertical sides and a rounded roof, the saplings forming the sides were bent in a continuous arc. These half-cylinders were shingled with bark or mats for six to eight related families. The design, called a Quonset hut during World War II, made a snug home for many American troops. A smaller, single-family wigwam with saplings bent in the same fashion would have a circular or an oval base. When it was time to move, the women would strip and carry the coverings to the next seasonal campground.

NORTHERN ALGONQUIAN "QUONSET" LONGHOUSE OF BARK AND A SINGLE-FAMILY WIGWAM OF SEWN MATS

Still farther north, the rectangular, straight-sided, Iroquois-style longhouses again appeared, along with the more temporary cone-shaped dwelling made for the single family. If need be, the birch-bark shingling could be carried to a new site. With the point aimed toward the sky, the cone-shaped home must have shed the snow easily. Most Coastal Algonquian villages were moved to a new spot every ten to twenty years. The gardens may have become overworked and sterile, firewood may have become exhausted, or the natives may have been forced by raiding tribes to find a more defensible location.

As a rule of thumb, the number of longhouses in each village indicated the emphasis placed on the clans. These permanent dwellings dominated the southern Coastal Algonquian villages. Like the southeastern Mississippian and the Iroquois tribes, the Coastal Algonquians' daily lives were focused around the extensive cultivated fields that were controlled by the women. And like those more settled tribes, the clans were matrilineal, with members related to each other through a female ancestor's bloodline.

On the other hand, the more mobile tribal villages with small, family-sized, and less permanent wigwams tended toward patrilineal clans. New situations and different seasonal and weather challenges in the more northerly reaches called for the leadership and protection of strong males. So it was, too, with their nomadic Paleo-American ancestors. Such was the gradual change from the mixed midcoastal clans to the patrilineal clans of the north. Whether matrilineal or patrilineal, the clans had considerable influence over village and tribal politics. They would be represented by the clan chiefs at the decision-making councils.

NORTHERN ALGONQUIAN TEPEE OF BIRCHBARK

ABBE MUSEUM, BAR HARBOR, MAINE

TRIBAL LEADERSHIP

Every tribal chieftain or sachem was selected from the same clan lineage as his predecessors. With the exception of the southern Atlantic tribes, the Algonquian sachems were democratic in their leadership ~ respected equals among equals. A woman could become a sachem if she was the wife of a deceased sachem without a son to inherit the position. At least it was so in Rhode Island's Narragansett tribe. Elsewhere in New England, history hints of "squaw sachems" who came to that office by descent. But male or female, they had little power over the people other than by persuasion.

He or she had no say over warriors planning a raid, but a male sachem's words would carry more weight if he had wisely and bravely led war parties into battle. He or she would be the go-between in local village disputes. The sachem would act as master of ceremonies at the various festivals and ceremonials occurring throughout the year and on occasion might even take the part of the village priest or shaman. The sachem presided over the village councils of wise men, elders, and clan heads. Each tribal village, then, had self-rule through its council representatives. When dealing with other tribes, the sachem was the spokesperson for his people. Such talks might concern intermarriage between tribes, common concerns over defense and war, agreements on hunting and fishing rights, and cooperation in hunting drives or sharing a harvest. Such meetings might lead to a loose confederacy, to the advantage of all.

The chieftains of the southern Coastal Algonquians were quite another story. It would seem that much of the Mayan-inspired southeastern Mississippian despotism had rubbed off on the tribes of North Carolina and Virginia. Each tribe had its king. At the time that Virginia's Powhatan inherited his chiefdom from his father, one of six villages below Richmond on the James River was palisaded against Siouan Mississippian raiders. From this stronghold he overran his Algonquian neighbors until he ruled over eight or nine thousand souls. He was as despotic as any of the Mayan-inspired Southern Cult chiefs, with the power of life or death over his subjects. Although John Smith's brush with death may have been but a symbolic part of a tribal adoption

WAMPANOAG KING PHILIP'S BALL-HEADED CLUB OF WOOD INLAID WITH WAMPUM BEADS AND SHELL.

POWHATAN'S BUCKSKIN MANTLE WITH SMALL SHELL DISCS - ASHMOLEAN MUSEUM, OXFORD

ceremony with Pocahontas in the lead role, enemy prisoners could expect no such happy ending.

Each Southern Algonquian minikingdom also had its class hierarchy that would please the ghosts of Mayan past. The chief, his family, and his fortunate relatives were automatically upper class members through inheritance. And as in the southeastern Mississippian tribes, any outstanding warrior, priest, respected spokesman and leader, or man who had amassed considerable wealth could join this select group. The chief's council of advisors was chosen from this upper crust, and together they made and regulated tribal guidelines. If a declaration of war was stalemated in council, the priests would have the deciding vote. Their contacts with the spirit world and their ability to interpret omens could forecast success or failure.

RELIGION

With minor variations, all the Algonquian peoples believed that the Great Spirit created the earth and its inhabitants. This conviction was long in place before any Christian missionaries ever set foot on American soil. To oversee his handiwork, the Great Spirit made lesser gods that included the Sun, Moon, Thunder, and Lightning in the form of a Thunderbird, Mother Earth, Fire, sea gods, and a host of others. These great supernatural powers could be contacted through visions and dreams by priests and shamans. It was prudent for all tribespeople to heed the wishes and advice of these supernatural beings and to give them the honor and thanks due to them with offerings such as the sacred tobacco. Failure to do so risked the visitation of the evil spirits.

Heading these malevolents was the twin brother of the Great Spirit. On the dark side of the spirit world, Evil Spirit delighted in bringing such miseries as floods, disease, poisonous snakes and plants, and just plain bad luck. Periodic thanksgiving ceremonies were pleasing to the benevolent spirits and would surely forestall those of evil intent. Scattered by the seasons as most Coastal Algonquians were, there were fewer occasions for thanksgiving gatherings than in the most permanent Iroquois towns. Likely there were those coastal Algonquians who felt a more frequent show of reverence might have prevented the Evil Spirit from bringing the European invaders who at first seemed to be gods in human form.

Minor spirits were everywhere in nature, be they stones, plants, trees, animals, or fish. The life of a woodland creature could be taken only in a time of necessity, when food or clothing was wanted. At the very least, a creature's distressed spirit deserved an apology in the form of prayer and perhaps tobacco. These countless supernatural forces were called manitous, and it was during the trances and dreams of the puberty isolation and

THESE NEW ENGLAND AMULETS WERE CHARMS THAT PROTECTED THE WEARER FROM EVIL AND INJURY.

and fasting ordeal (see page 65) that a boy or girl discovered his or her guardian spirit. With this mystical backing, one could find direction in life and encouragement in reaching one's goals. Wearing the manitou's special amulet would ward off misfortune and illness. Every tribesperson should have a secret and sacred medicine bundle. Secure in a deerskin pouch would be the objects that had been revealed in the fasting visions during the search for a personal manitou. These might include a meaningful feather, a stone crystal, or a magical effigy and were not meant for prying eyes. Through them, the owner could contact the manitou's spirit for insight, assistance, and strength.

RARE REPRESENTATION OF A MANITOU CARVED OVER THE DOOR OF A DELAWARE HOUSE BEFORE 1731 - AFTER A SKETCH BY ANDREW HESSELIUS (BIÖRCK 1731:27)

A tribesperson must never forget that the manitou guardians were counterbalanced by the Evil Spirit and his worrisome underlings. Ancient tribal legends tell of mischievous, elflike people, fearful monsters, demons, witches, and ghosts of the dead. To blunt their ill will, the priest-healers must be consulted. With their special powers they could contact the lesser gods for advice. The shaman or medicine man might be a conjurer who could call on these supernatural forces to cast out the bodily miseries caused by the evil ones. He would be akin to a magician, and his curing ritual might include "shooting," or magically propelling, a white shell or sucking out a feather through a tube — either one being the cause of the symptoms. On the other hand, there was the traditional physician who used a wide variety of herbs and powders and set bones. Chances were that both curative approaches were used by one and the same healer.

COPPER THUNDERBIRD FROM NEW HAMPSHIRE- PEABODY MUSEUM, HARVARD UNIVERSITY

The Algonquians had medical societies somewhat similar to the Iroquoian False Faces. Periodically they drove disease from the village. Village sweat lodges were frequented for the steaming and sweating out of bodily ills and for refreshing the mind. As with the Delaware, there would often be separate steam baths for men and women at either end of the village near a stream. In the New England tribes, men, women, and children would be together. Water was poured on the red-hot stones in the hearth to produce something of a human clambake. After being well steamed, the people would plunge into the stream, or, in wintertime, would roll in the snow.

SEATED-BEAR EFFIGY FROM SALEM, MASSACHUSETTS PEABODY MUSEUM, SALEM, MASSACHUSETTS

WARFARE

Intertribal warfare in the Late Woodland Period was ongoing for a variety of reasons — to avenge insults or injuries to a clan member, to extract tributes, to secure more women, to repel Iroquois attacks against an Algonquian

CHEROKEE EFFIGY PIPE FROM NORTH CAROLINA. INDIAN NOTES VOL. 1, 1928, pp. 318~320

LENAPE "TOMAHAWK" ~ A WORD ADOPTED
BY THE EARLY JAMESTOWN SETTLERS
ASHMOLEAN MUSEUM, OXFORD

SENECA WARCLUB OF HARDWOOD WITH
INCISED DESIGNS AND RUBBED WITH RED OCHER
"INDIAN NOTES" JAN. 1926 No.1

confederacy member, or to appropriate fertile lands, shellfish beds
and prime hunting lands belonging
to neighbors. From the age of five
or six, boys practiced their marksmanship with bows and arrows, stalked small
game, or waited in ambush along a game trail.

Hunting down an enemy wouldn't be all that different.
He would hone his aggressiveness in village games in
preparation for the day when he would be one of those
in the war party. His village status might well de-
pend on his daring and bravery. When the big moment
came, all eyes would be on him as he joined the war
dance, face and body painted in bold designs that should
give any enemy second thoughts.

Each Coastal Algonquian warrior would certainly
have in hand his 3-to-6-foot-long bow, usually of hickory,
ash, beech, rock maple, witch hazel, or black locust. The
nocks were strung with a doubled strip of sinew that
had been rolled and twisted. Triangular stone points with
concave bases were lashed to the arrow shafts with strands
of sinew. Other arrowhead materials used were bone deer
antler, horseshoe crab tails, and eagle claws. Two spiral or,
more commonly, three straight feathers were fletched on
the shaft near the colored designs that marked the owner.

They were carried in a quiver
at the back of the shoulder, and
were grasped with the opposite
hand. The quivers could be made
of animal skin, hide, rush, or the halves
of a wooden cylinder scooped out and
lashed together.

The warrior would also carry a
ball-headed club armed with a stone
blade or sometimes an armed, sword-
shaped club. In addition, he might be
protected by a shield of moose rawhide, bark, or wood, and occasionally
a chest armor of several thickness of
rawhide, which no arrow could penetrate ~ hopefully.

As elsewhere in the northeastern
woodlands, the attacks were com-
mando style. Early morning would catch
an enemy village asleep. They might

A NORTH CAROLINA CHIEFTAIN ~
THIS 1590 DE BRY ENGRAVING IS FROM
JOHN WHITE'S WATERCOLOR SERIES.

DELAWARE BOW WITH CARVED DECORATIONS
THE BRITISH MUSEUM, LONDON

then be taken by surprise, particularly if the village wasn't stockaded or given warning by its dogs. Most raids were small scale, with no more than seven or eight warriors losing their lives. Women and children captives were often brought back for adoption, and it has been said that the chastity of women captives was never violated. Warrior prisoners had a chance at life if their heads or scalps were still in place and they could successfully run the gauntlet between the two rows of villagers wielding sticks and clubs. If the prisoner was no longer standing at the end of his run, he'd best get his warrior chant in tune and courage ready for the torture and the slow death that was sure to follow.

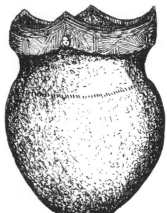

CAPE COD POT OF
IROQUOIS DESIGN

VILLAGE LIFE

Seasonal rounds were much like those of their Central Algonquian brothers, as noted on pages 60~64. So too was growing up in the village (pages 64~66). Puberty and marriage, however, had some minor variations. When a girl had her first menses, she would be confined to the same hut that she had been delivered in. Taboos included not touching her hair or food with her hands. Once back with her family, she might advertise her marriageability, as did the Delaware young women, by wearing wampum or partially covering her head.

The Algonquians married at an early age. Women would be in their midteens and their husbands a bit older, say seventeen or eighteen. The age difference allowed a young man to prove himself a good provider. Only then would his mother go shopping for a suitable bride in a different clan. The prospective couple would meet under the watchful eye of a chaperone. If the woman didn't like what she saw, she could send the suitor on his way. But if romance was in the air, the man could make points with her family by bringing them a deer or some lesser game. If there were no hitches during the waiting period, the village would have a new husband and wife. As elsewhere in the woodlands, marriages were usually monogamous, and adultery was not an option.

PENNACOOK POUCH,
MID-SEVENTEENTH CENTURY
PEABODY MUSEUM, SALEM, MASSACHUSETTS

EIGHTEENTH-CENTURY DRINKING CUP WITH A FOX EFFIGY
AND BELT TOGGLE, NEW ENGLAND ALGONQUIAN INDIANS
WORCESTER HISTORICAL MUSEUM, MASSACHUSETTS

DEATH

There was a time for every villager when his or her seasonal rounds must end. Coastal Algonquians could face death without fear, for the end of life on earth was not the work of the Evil Spirit or his malevolent creations. Instead, the spirit of the deceased would live forever in the southwestern world of the Great Spirit. If an earthen burial was impossible in the frozen ground of winter, the body was placed on a scaffold until warmer weather. Probably family and friends made the burial arrangements instead of moieties and dual divisions, which was the custom in the rest of the northeastern woodlands. Usually the bark- or mat-wrapped body would be placed in an earthen grave in a flexed position. The head would be pointed toward his or her final destination in the southwestern sky.

For the journey, a man's prized and practical bow and arrows, stone axe, and knife would be placed by his side along with his pipe, tobacco, and his wealth in wampum. A woman would be accompanied by her favorite pottery, baskets, and a mortar and pestle for use in the spirit world. She would be dressed in her best clothing with her bead necklace as a finishing touch.

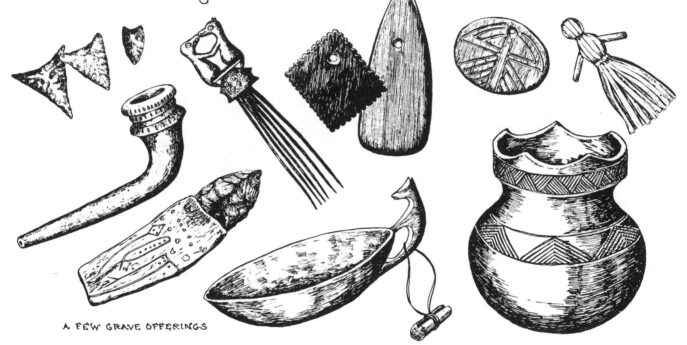

A FEW GRAVE OFFERINGS

The Algonquians generally believed that everyone had two souls. The Heart Soul remained near the burial site for eleven days. During that time, food was placed by the grave site so that the Heart Soul could sustain itself on the food spirits. On the twelfth day, a Feast of the Dead was offered to send it off on its journey to the Great Spirit. But if the person had been a murderer, thief, or liar in life, he would spend eternity wandering aimlessly in space.

On the other hand, the Blood Soul must forever remain on earth. If the burial rituals or the Feast of the Dead had been improper or ignored, the Blood spirit would come in the darkness of night and haunt those responsible. This fearful ghost could inflict injury and illness upon the guilty. Because of this, no right-thinking villager would dare to eat in the dark or allow an ill person to remain in a dark dwelling.

The common folk of the North Carolina and Virginia Algonquian tribes could count on being laid to rest in earthen graves. But in these southern reaches where the Mississippian cults had considerable influence, the privileged upper classes could expect extraordinary rites. Their dead were laid out on a mat-covered scaffold within the village temple. The skin was carefully cut free and removed intact. The remaining flesh was excised from the bones, sun-dried, and then wrapped in mats at the feet of the skeleton. The skin was then padded and sewn back over the bony form to give a lifelike appearance. For this curious ritual there were official bonepickers in the Choctau tribe. These Mississippian specialists actually grew lengthy fingernails to better deflesh the bodies.

Priests kept a perpetual fire burning in the temple much like the Temple Mound cults and prayed day and night over the VIP bodies. Their lives in the afterworld depended on priestly intercession. Carved wooden idols representing many gods watched over the proceedings. The evil and vengeful god, called Oke, must be given offerings of tobacco, copper objects, and bead wampum to blunt his mischief to the departed. Even if excluded from such death benefits, all the southeastern Algonquians believed they would also have life after death. Reincarnation, whether or not representing the Blood Soul returning to the earth in human form, seems to be a common theme throughout the southeast.

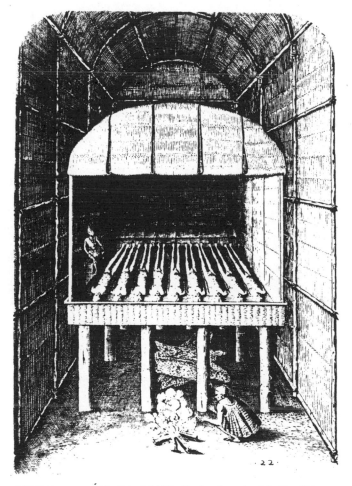

AN IDOL WATCHES OVER THE SKIN-COVERED SKELETONS OF THE CHIEFTAINS WHILE A PRIEST KEEPS CONSTANT VIGIL BELOW.   DE BRY ENGRAVING, 1590

85

SHORT BACKWARD GLANCES

One of the greatest adventures on earth began in the far reaches of prehistory — probably as early as 30,000 B.C. Quite by happenstance, one or more family bands of Asian hunters were tracking their Ice Age quarry near the Siberian Arctic Circle. Frigid winds had converted volumes of sea moisture into a massive buildup of glaciers. As ocean levels dropped, the Bering Strait seabed became a flat, grassed-over pathway connecting Asia with Alaska. Man and beast could pass freely until a warming trend again drowned the connection. The few families who ventured across had become Paleo-American Indians. Without fanfare or perhaps even knowing they were then part of a vast, uninhabited new continent, the nomadic big-game hunters wandered into every corner of their new home.

By 12,000 B.C. the continued warmth had chased the glaciers northward and the cold-loving animals were fast disappearing. In the vast woodlands between the Mississippi River and the Atlantic coastline, nut-bearing hardwoods nudged their way into the evergreen stands by 8000 B.C. to provide food for the smaller animals that lunched on the varied fare. The Late Archaic Period had begun, and the scattered bands settled down within this immense area that offered foraging and good hunting.

The passage of two thousand years brought the Middle Archaic Period and notable changes in the settled family bands. Each had prospered and multiplied within its own lands. The first steps toward tribal unity began with interband marriages and the occasional joining with neighbors for common concerns and protection from marauders. There was even leisure for dressing up with ornaments and for the deeper concerns over life after the grave.

The tribal concept had its beginnings during the Late Archaic Period between 4000 and 1000 B.C. when the primitive Algonquian Muskhogean language divided into separate tongues. The Muskhogean speakers of the southeastern woodlands could unify their customs and traditions, as did the Algonquian speakers, as did the Algonquian speakers who inhabited the northeast. But deep in the Algonquian territory, pre-Iroquoian nonconformists went their own way with a different speech. More would be heard from these independent people in the future. Meanwhile, there developed three important northeastern cultures: the Narrow Point, the Lake Forest, and the Maritime.

The Narrow Point culture, otherwise known as the Mast Forest Archaics, certainly comprised the largest number of Algonquian peoples. We know them for their unique narrow atlatl dart points with squared bases. Their snug dwellings resembled a snail's shell and are the earliest yet discovered. Their fishing weirs were highlighted by discoveries made during Boston's subway excavations. Otherwise we have much to learn about these Late Archaic Indians.

A second Algonquian culture, the Lake Forest Indians, was located around the Great Lakes region. These freshwater fishing specialists worked the waters in dugout canoes with an array of gillnets, seins, harpoons, gaffs, and three-pronged spears. It was along the shores of Lake Superior that a wealth of pure copper nuggets was discovered. Craftspeople found that by repeatedly heating the chunks between poundings, brittleness and cracking could be avoided. The variety of useful tools made by these so-called "Old Copper Culture" Late Archaics was eagerly sought by traders throughout the northeastern Woodlands.

The third culture, the Maritime Indians, was not of Algonquian origins. Probably they were descendants of those Paleo-American hunters who had continued their Ice Age game hunt into the far north. They had reversed direction by migrating down from Labrador into the Canadian Maritime Provinces and on into central Maine. Because the Maritimers sprinkled their gravesites with red-ocher powder that resembled life-giving blood, they are also known as the Red Paint People. In their obsession with afterlife in the spirit world, they provided the dead with fine effigy sculptures, fragile slate spearheads practical only among the spirits, fire-making sets, and woodworking tools of rare and colorful stone. The Maritime Indians' reverence for life after death spilled over into the entire Algonquian northeast with profound and ongoing effects.

The Maritimers had not ignored the good eating that the sea provided. They fished with hook and sinker and net from dugout canoes. They took on seals, walruses, porpoises, and even whales with barbed and toggled harpoons. It is surprising that no interest was taken in the profusion of shellfish in shallower waters.

When the Terminal Period, from 2000 to 1000 B.C., came to the woodlands, the good life seemed to be everywhere. Now united with common language, customs, traditions, and the Maritimer's promise of life hereafter, a much appreciated household necessity eased the cooking chores: Soft soapstone could be crafted into pots for brewing stews and the cups and plates for serving them.

With such advances, the rumblings coming from the pre-Iroquoian villages seemed of little importance. And trouble there was in this problem pocket, for villagers were not only battling among themselves but also spreading the fighting to the neighboring Lake Forest tribes. These Algonquians fled for their lives to the east. Those who sought refuge in the lands of the Maritime Indians would become the Micmac, Maliseet, and Abenaki tribes. They were the likely originators of the birchbark canoe, and, judging from the shell middens that remained, they certainly appreciated the shellfish that the Maritimers had left untouched.

The Early Woodland Period that began by 1000 B.C. held the promise of even greater advances and luxuries. The Adena who lived in the Ohio River valleys had taken the Maritime graveside ceremonials to heart. In their religious fervor they constructed large earthen mounds to hold their red ocher-sprinkled dead. Their grave goods were enviable works of art—so much so that a lively trade for them developed among the other Algonquian tribes. The Adena missionary-traders also introduced the all-important discoveries that common clay could be baked into all manner of containers and that cultivation could overcome the uncertainties of foraging.

The Hopewells, the later generation of the Ohio Adenas, upstaged their ancestors with their bigger and better mounds and exotic grave offerings. By 300 B.C. their missionary-traders were searching most of North America for the very finest and most unusual of raw materials. In exchange they offered wondrous grave goods that would have amazed the Adenas, and this time they concentrated on the southeastern Woodland tribes. Wealth flowed back to the chieftains, priests, craftspeople, and the inevitable middleman. Relatives of this fortunate few took such pride in being of the same blood that the clan concept took hold.

When the Late Woodland Period opened in A.D. 700, new ideas were flowing into the southeastern woodlands from Central American Mayans. Already caught up in the Hopewell burial mounds and a taste for their handsomely crafted grave offerings, the southerners fell under the Mayan spell. The middle Mississippi Valley became a showplace of large cities dominated by huge earthen temple mounds that resembled the stone-temple pyramids of Mexico. The ceremonial plazas and fine art were also imitated, as, unfortunately, was the oppressive caste system.

Throughout the southeast a religious cult took firm hold. Powerful priests followed the human sacrificial ceremonies in the Mayan manner. Known as the Southern Cult, they could boast of such religious trappings as symbolic motifs, sacrificial knives, stone statues and effigies, masks, and ceremonial axes and maces. The privileged few continued their heavy-handed rule until the coming of the European armies in the sixteenth century.

Efforts to Mayanize the northeastern Woodland tribes had little success. The Algonquians were happy enough to continue the traditions passed on by the Maritime Late Archaics and the Adena-Hopewells. Meanwhile, the hotbed of Iroquois sandwiched between the Central and Coastal Algonquians were still decimating themselves with inter-tribal clan feuds. Fortunately, wiser heads prevailed and the great League of the Iroquois brought intertribal peace through council repre-sentation. Unfortunately, this warrior society could then turn its fury on the peaceloving Woodland tribes. Little wonder many eagerly sought the protection of the incoming European colonists.

By the early sixteenth century, the Late Woodland Period had come to an end ~ along with many Woodland Indian customs and traditions as well. After many millennia of isolation, the woodland tribes of the Maritime Provinces met the first European fishermen. It happened well before Columbus's discoveries and the countless explorers, trad-ers, and colonists who followed. The Stone Age tribespeople were overwhelmed by the newcomers, awed by their technology and trade goods, riddled with foreign diseases to which they had no immunity, felled by muskets and alcohol, and were gradually herded onto reservations that seemed of little value to lawmakers.

To end on a happier note, it should be mentioned that many of the pre-contact customs and traditions of the woodland peoples are still being practiced. Their descendants ~ and their fellow Americans as well ~ are developing a new awareness of their ancient and colorful past. You might like to become better acquainted with the following museums and their displays on the Woodland Indians of North America.

MUSEUMS CONTAINING DISPLAYS

In addition to the following museums featuring American Indian artifacts, many historical societies and county and natural-history museums have outstanding Native American exhibits among their varied collections.

ALABAMA

Alabama Museum of Natural History, Smith Hall, University of Alabama, Tuscaloosa, AL 35487-0340

Anniston Museum of Natural History, 800 Museum, Drive, Anniston, AL 36202

Bessemer Hall of History, 1905 Alabama Ave., Bessemer, AL 35020

Horseshoe Bend National Military Park, Alabama Hwy. 49 at Tallapoosa River, Daviston, AL 36256

Red Mountain Museum, A Location of Discovery 2000, 1421 22nd St., Birmingham, AL 35205

Russell Cave National Monument, 3729 County Rd. 98, Bridgeport, AL 35740

Thomas E. McMillan Museum, Jefferson Davis College, 220 Alco Dr., Brewton, AL 36426

ARKANSAS

Arkansas Museum of Science and History, MacArthur Park, Little Rock, AR 72202

Arkansas State University Museum, Museum Bldg., 100 Cooley Dr., Jonesboro, AR 72401

Hampson Museum State Park, Lake Dr. at Hwy. 61, Wilson, AR 72395

Henderson state University Museum, The Stone House, Henderson & 10th, Arkadelphia, AR 71999-0001

Ka-Do-Ha Indian Discovery Museum, P.O. Box 669, Murfreesboro, AR 71958

Old Washington Historic State Park, Franklin St., Washington, AR 71862

Toltec Mounds Archaeological State Park, 490 Toltec Mounds Rd., Hwy. 165 S., Scott, AR 72142

The University Museum, University of Arkansas, Museum Bldg. Rm. 202, Fayetteville, AR 72701

CONNECTICUT

The Bruce Museum, Museum Dr., Greenwich, CT 06830

The Institute for American Indian Studies, 38 Curtis Rd., P.O. Box 1260, Washington Green, CT 06793-0260

New Britain Youth Museum, 30 High St., New Britain, CT 06051

Peabody Museum of Natural History, Yale University, 170 Whitney Ave., New Haven, CT 06520-8118

Tantaquidgeon Indian Museum, Rte. 32, Norwich-New London Rd., Uncasville, CT 06382

DISTRICT OF COLUMBIA

Explorers Hall National Geographic Society, 1145 17th St. N.W., Washington, DC 20036

Indian Arts and Crafts Board (contemporary art), 1849 C St. N.W., Rm. 4004-MIB, U.S. Dept. of Interior, Washington, DC 20240

National Museum of Natural History, 10th St. at 6 Constitution Ave., N.W., Washington, DC 20560

United States Department of the Interior Museum, 1849 C Street, N.W., Washington, DC 20240

FLORIDA

Crystal River State Archaeological Site, 3400 N. Museum Pt., Crystal River, FL 32629

Florida Community College, Kent State

Campus Museum/Gallery, 3939 Roosevelt
Blvd., Jacksonville, FL 32205

Graves Museum of Archaeology and Natural
History, 408 S. Federal Hwy., Dania, FL
33004

Historic Spanish Point, 500 N. Tamiami Trail,
Osprey, FL 34229

Indian Temple Mound Museum, 139
Miraclestrip Parkway, S.E., Fort Walton
Beach, FL 32549

The Museum of Arts and Sciences, Inc.,
1040 Museum Blvd., Daytona Beach, FL
32114

San Marcos De Apalache State Historic Site,
Canal St., P.O. Box 27, St. Marks, FL
32355

South Florida Museum & Bishop
Planetarium, 201 10th St., W. Bradenton,
FL 34025

GEORGIA

Chattahoochee River National Recreation
Area, 1978 Indian Ford Parkway,
Dunwood, GA 30350

Etowah Indian Mounds Historical Site, 813
Indian Mounds Rd., S.W., Cartersville, GA
30120

Indian Springs State Park Museum, Hwy. 42,
5 mi. S. of Jackson, Flovilla, GA 30216

Kolomoki Mounds State Park Museum, Rt. 1,
Blakely, GA 31723

Ocmulgee National Monument, 1207 Emery
Hwy., Macon, GA 31201

University of Georgia Museum of Natural
History, Natural History Bldg., University
of Georgia, Athens, GA 30602-1882

ILLINOIS

The Anthropology Museum, Northern Illinois
University, DeKalb, IL 60115

Black Hawk State Historic Site: Hauberg
Indian Museum, Illinois Rte. 5, Rock
Island, IL 61201

Cahokia Mounds State Historic Site, 30
Ramey St., East St. Louis, IL 62201

Dickson Mounds Museum, Lewiston, IL
61542

Field Museum of Natural History, Roosevelt
Rd. at Lake Shore Dr., Chicago, IL 60605

Kampsville Archaeological Museum, Oak St.,
Kampsville, IL 62053

The Mitchell Indian Museum at Kendall
College, 2408 Orrington Ave., Evanston,
IL 60201

Schingoethe Center for Native American
Cultures, 347 S. Gladstone, Aurora
University, Dunham Hall, Aurora, IL
60506-4892

Starved Rock State Park, Box 116, Utica, IL
61373

University Museum, Southern Illinois
University, Carbondale, IL 62901-4508

INDIANA

Angel Mounds Historic Site, 8215 Pollack
Ave., Evansville, IN 47715

Eiteljorg Museum of the American Indians
and Western Art, 500 W. Washington,
Indianapolis, IN 46204

IOWA

Effigy Mounds National Monument, 151
Highway 76, Harpers Ferry, IA 52146

Putnam Museum of History & Natural
Science, 1717 W. 12th St., Davenport, IA
52804

Sanford Museum and Planetarium, 117 E.
Willow St., Cherokee, IA 51012

KENTUCKY

Museum of Anthropology, University Drive,
Northern Kentucky University, Highland
Heights, KY 41099-6210

Wickliffe Mounds, 94 Green St., Wickliffe,
KY 42087

LOUISIANA

Louisiana Tech Museum, Louisiana Tech University, Ruston, LA 71272

MAINE

Abbe Museum, Sieur de Monts Spring, Acadia National Park, Bar Harbor, ME 04609

Colonial Pemaquid, Colonial Pemaquid State Park, New Harbor, ME 04554

Hudson Museum, University of Maine, 5476 Maine Center for the Arts, Orono, ME 04469-5746

MARYLAND

St. Clements Island-Potomac River Museum, Breezepoint Rd., Colton Point, MD 20626

MASSACHUSETTS

Fruitlands Museums, 102 Prospect Hill Rd., Harvard, MA 01451

The Mission House, Main St., Stockbridge, MA 01262

Peabody Essex Museum, E. India Square, Salem, MA 01970

Peabody Museum of Archaeology & Ethnology, 11 Divinity Ave., Cambridge, MA 02138

Plimoth Plantation Inc., Warren Ave., Plymouth, MA 02362

Robbins Museum of Archaeology, 17 Jackson St., Middleborough, MA 02346-0700

Robert S. Peabody Museum of Archaeology, 175 Main St., Andover, MA 01810

Springfield Science Museum, 236 State St., Springfield, MA 01103

MICHIGAN

Andrew J. Blackbird Museum, 368 E. Main St., Harbor Springs, MI 49740

Chippewa Nature Center, 400 S. Badour Rd.;

Rt. 9, Midland, MI 48640

Isle Royale National Park, 800 E. Lakeshore Dr., Houghton, MI 49931

Jesse Besser Museum, 491 Johnson St., Alpena, MI 49707

Mackinac Island State Park Commission, Mackinac Island, MI 49757

Teysen's Woodland Indian Museum, 415 W. Huron Ave., Mackinaw City, MI 49701

University of Michigan Museum of Anthropology, 4009 Ruthven Museums Bldg., Ann Arbor, MI 48109

Wayne State University Museum of Anthropology, 6001 Cass Ave., Detroit, MI 48202

MINNESOTA

Evelyn Payne Hatcher Museum of Anthropology, Rm. 213 A Stewart Hall, St. Cloud University, St. Cloud, MN 56301

Minnesota Historical Society's Grand Mound History Center, Rte. 7, Box 453, International Falls, MN 56649

Pipestone County Historical Museum, 113 S. Hiawatha, Pipestone, MN 56164

Walker Wildlife and Indian Artifacts Museum, State Hwy. 200, Walker, MN 56484

Winnebago Area Museum, 18 1st Ave., N.E., Winnebago, MN 56098

MISSISSIPPI

Cobb Institute of Archaeology, Drawer AR, Mississippi State University, MS 39762

Cottonlandia Museum, Hwy. 82W., Greenwood, MS 38930

Grand Village of the Natchez Indians, 400 Jefferson Davis Blvd., Natchez, MS 39120

MISSOURI

Battle of Carthage State Historic Site, East Chestnut, Lamar, MO 64863

Fort Osage Historic Site, 105 Osage St.,

Sibley, MO 64088

Graham Cave State Park, N. Outer Rd., Montgomery City, MO 63361

Maramec Museum, The James Foundation, Maramec Spring Park, St. James, MO 65559

Museum of Anthropology, University of Missouri, 104 Swallow Hall, University of Missouri, Columbia, MO 65211

Van Meter State Park, Rte. 122, Miami, MO 65344

NEW HAMPSHIRE

Libby Museum, Rt. 109 N., Wolfeboro, NH 03894

NEW JERSEY

Seton Hall University Museum, S. Orange Ave., South Orange, NJ 07079

NEW YORK

Akwesasne Museum, Rte. 37, Hogansburg, NY 13655

Iroquois Indian Museum, Caverns Rd., P.O. Box 7, Howes Cave, NY 12049

The Museums at Hartwick, Hartwick College, Oneonta, NY 13820-4020

National Museum of the American Indian, Smithsonian Institution, 3753 Broadway at 155th St., New York, NY 10032-1596

Native American Center for the Living Arts, 25 Rainbow Blvd. S., Niagara Falls, NY 14303

New York State Archaeological Association, 657 East Ave., Box 1480, Rochester, NY 14603-1480

Owasco Teyetasta, Emerson Park, Auburn, NY 13021

Sainte Marie Among the Iroquois, P.O. Box 146, Liverpool, NY 13088

Seneca–Iroquois National Museum, Broad St. Ext., Allegany Indian Reservation, Salamanca, NY 14779

Six Nations Indian Museum, Roakdale Road, HCR #1, Box 10, Onchiota, NY 12968

Southold Indian Museum, Bayview Rd., Southold, NY 11971

NORTH CAROLINA

Frisco Native American Museum and Natural History Center, Box 399, Hwy. 12, Frisco, NC 27936

Indian Museum of the Carolinas, Inc., 607 Turnpike Rd., Laurinburg, NC 28352

Mountain Heritage Center, Western Carolina University, Cullowhee, NC 28723

Museum of Anthropology, Wake Forest Dr., Winston-Salem, NC 27109-7267

Museum of the Cherokee Indian, U.S. 441, Cherokee, NC 28719

Native American Resource Center, Pembroke State University, College Rd., Pembroke, NC 28372

Town Creek Indian Mound State Historic Site, Montgomery County Rd. 1542, Mount Gilead, NC 27306

OHIO

Dayton Museum of Natural History, 2600 DeWeese Pkwy., Dayton, OH 45414

Flint Ridge State Memorial Museum, 7091 Brownsville Rd. S.E., Glenford, OH 43739-9609

Fort Ancient Museum, 6123 St., Rt. 350, exit 32 & 36 off I–71, Oregonia, OH 45054

Gnadenhutten Historical Park & Museum, S. Cherry St. & County Rd. 10, Gnadenhutten, OH 44629

Hopewell Culture National Historic Park, 16062 State Route 104, Chillicothe, OH 45601-8694

Indian Museum of Lake County Ohio, c/o Lake Erie College, 391 W. Washington, Painesville, OH 44077

Moundbuilders State Memorial & Museum,

99 Cooper Ave., Newark, OH 43055
Ohio Historical Center, 1982 Velma Ave.,
Columbus, OH 43211-2497
Serpent Mound Museum, 3850 State Rte. 73,
Peebles, OH 45660

PENNSYLVANIA

**University of Pennsylvania Museum of
Archaeology & Anthropology,** 33rd &
Spruce Sts., Philadelphia, PA 19104-6324

RHODE ISLAND

Haffenreffer Museum of Anthropology,
Brown University, Mt. Hope Grant, Tower
St., Bristol, RI 02809-4050
Museum of Primitive Art and Culture, 1058
Kingstown Rd., Peace Dale, RI 02883
Rhode Island Historical Society, 110
Benevolent St., Providence, RI 02906
**Roger Williams Park Museum of Natural
History,** Roger Williams Park, Providence,
RI 02905

SOUTH CAROLINA

Museum of York County, 4621 Mount
Gallant Rd., Rock Hill, SC 29732-9905
**South Carolina Institute of Archaeology &
Anthropology,** 1321 Pendleton St.,
University of South Carolina, Columbia,
SC 29208

TENNESSEE

C.H. Nash Museum–Chucalissa, 1987 Indian
Village Dr., Memphis, TN 38109
Frank H. McClung Museum, University of
Tennessee, 1327 Circle Park Dr., Knoxville,
TN 37996-3200
Pinson Mounds State Archaeological Area,
460 Ozier Rd., Pinson, TN 38366
Red Clay Historical Park, 1140 Red Clay
Park Rd., S.W., Cleveland, TN 37311

VERMONT

Robert Hull Fleming Museum, University of
Vermont, Colchester Ave., Burlington, VT
05405

VIRGINIA

Prince William Forest Park, Rte. 619,
Triangle, VA 22172
Ramsay Nature Center, 5700 Sanger Ave.,
Alexandria, VA 22311

WEST VIRGINIA

Delf Norona Museum & Culture Center, 801
Jefferson Ave., Moundsville, WV 26041

WISCONSIN

Aztalan Museum, N. 6264 Highway Q,
Jefferson, WI 53549
Chief Oshkosh Museum, 7631 Egg Harbor
Rd., Egg Harbor, WI 54209
Logan Museum of Anthropology, Prospect
and Bushnell, Beloit, WI 53511
Oneida Nation Museum/Cultural Center, W.
892 EE Cty. Trk. Rd., De Pere, WI 54115
Thunderbird Museum, Hatfield N9517
Thunderbird Lane, Merrillan, WI 54754-
8033

BIBLIOGRAPHY

Adney, Edwin Tappan, and Howard I. Chapelle. *The Bark Canoes and Skin Boats of North America Museum of History and Technology.* U.S. Government Printing Office, 1964.

Armbruster, Eugene L. *The Indians of New England and New Netherland.* Limited Edition 1918.

Barbour, Philip L. *Pocahontas And Her World.* Houghton, Mifflin, Boston, 1970.

Baxter, Rev. Joseph. *Journal of Several Visits to the Indians on the Kennebec River, 1717.* David Clapp & Son, Boston, 1867.

Bierer, Bert W. *Indians and Artifacts in the Southeast.* Bierer Publishing, Columbia, 1980.

Borns, Howard W., Jr. "Possible Paleo-Indian Migration Routes in the Northeast." MAS 34, nos. 1 and 2 (1972–73): 13–15.

Bourque, Bruce J., Maine State Museum and Bates College, "Ethnicity on the Maritime Peninsula 1600–1750." *Ethnohistory* 36, no. 3 (1989): 257–84.

Bourque, Bruce J., and Ruth Holmes Whitehead. "Torrentines and the Introduction of European Trade Goods in the Gulf of Maine" *Ethnohistory* 32, no.4: 327–41.

Bishop, Carl Whiting. *Man From the Farthest Past.* Volume Seven of the Smithsonian Institution Series. New York, 1930, 1934, 1938, 1943.

Burland, Cottie. *North American Indian Mythology.* Hamlyn Publishing Group, London, 1975.

Burrage, Henry S., ed. *Early English and French Voyages.* Charles Scribner's Sons, New York, 1906.

Bushnell, G.H.S. *The First Americans: The Pre-Columbian Civilization.* McGraw Hill, New York, 1968.

Champlain, Samuel de. *Voyages of Samuel de Champlain 1604–1618.* Edited by W. I. Grant. New York, 1907.

Chrisman, Donald, MacNeish, Richard S., Mavalwala, Jamshed, and Howard Savage. "Pre-Clovis Human Friction Skin Prints From Pendejo Cave, New Mexico." Unpublished.

Congdon, Isabelle P. *Indian Tribes of Maine.* The Brunswick Publishing Company, Brunswick, Maine, 1961.

Constable, George, and the Editors of Time-Life Books, *The Emergence of Man: The Neanderthals.* Time-Life Books, New York, 1973.

Davidson, Daniel Sutherland. *Snowshoes.* American Philosophical Society, Philadelphia, 1937.

Denton, Daniel, "Of New York, Formerly Called New Netherlands . . ." *The Bulletin of the Historical Society of Pennsylvania* 1 (1848): 1–15.

Early Man in America. Readings from *Scientific American.* W. H. Freeman, San Francisco, 1968.

Ettwein, Rev. John. "Remarks Upon the Traditions & C. of the Indians of North America." *The Bulletin of the Historical Society of Pennsylvania* 1, no. 3 (1848): 29–43.

Favour, Edith. "Indian Games, Toys, And Pastimes Of Maine And The Maritimes" Bulletin X, The Robert Abbe Museum, Bar Harbor, 1974.

Fernald, Peggy, and Alice N. Wellman. "Brief Description of Birch Bark Canoe Building." Maine Coast Printers, Rockland, 1970.

Fetchko, Peter, John Grimes, and William Phippen. *Stone Age New England: 10,000 Years of History.* Peabody Museum of Salem, Mass., 1976.

Folsom, Franklin. *America's Ancient Treasures.* Rand McNally, New York, 1971.

Fowler, William S. *A Handbook of Indian Artifacts from Southern New England.* Edited by Jean-Jacques Rivard. The Massachusetts Archaeological Society, 1976.

———. *Bulletin of the Massachusetts Archaeological Society* 34, nos. 3 and 4 (1973): 1–12, 15–22.

———. "Archaic Discoveries at Flat River." *Bulletin of the Massachusetts Archaeological Society* 29, no. 2 (1968): 17–36.

Fowler, William Smith. *Ten Thousand Years In America.* Vantage Press, New York, 1957.

Gowlett, John A. J. *Ascent to Civilization: The Archaeology of Early Man.* Alfred A. Knopf, New York, 1985.

Gridley, Marion E. *America's Indian Statues.* The Amerindian Towertown Press, Chicago, 1966.

Griffin, James B., ed. *Archaeology of Eastern United States.* University of Chicago Press, 1952.

Gringhuis, Dirk. "Indian Costume at Mackinac: Seventeenth and Eighteenth Century." *Mackinac History* 2, no. 1 (1972).

Hadlock, Wendell S., and Eva L. Butler. "Uses of Birch Bark in the Northeast." Robert Abbe Museum, Bulletin No. 7. Bar Harbor, Maine, 1957.

Hamilton, T. M. *Native American Bows.* George Shumway Publishers, New York, 1972.

Hamm, Kim, *Bows & Arrows of the Native Americans.* Lyons & Burford, New York, and Bois d'Arc Press, Azle, Texas, 1991.

Heye, George G. "Wampum Collection." *Indian Notes* 7 (1930): 320–24.

Howell, F. Clark, and the Editors of Time-Life Books. *Early Man.* Time-Life Books, New York, 1965, 1970, 1972.

Huden, John C., comp. *Archaeology In Vermont.* Rev. ed. Charles E. Tuttle, Rutland, VT., 1971.

Hudson, Charles. *The Southeastern Indians.* University of

Tennessee Press, Knoxville, 1976.

Hunter, William A. "The Ohio, the Indian Land." *Pennsylvania History* 21, no. 4 (1954).

Irwin, R. Stephen. *Hunters of the Eastern Forest.* Hancock House, Surrey, B.C., and Washington, 1984.

Jefferson, Thomas. *Notes on the State of Virginia.* Edited by William Peden. University of North Carolina Press, 1954; W.W. Norton & Company, New York and London, 1972.

Jennings, Jesse, D. *Prehistory of North America.* Second edition, McGraw Hill, New York, 1968.

———. *Prehistory of North America.* Third edition. Mayfield Publishing, Mountain View, Calif., 1989.

Jennings, Jesse D., and Edward Norbeck, eds. *Prehistoric Man in the New World.* University of Chicago Press, 1960.

Johanson, Donald, and Naitland Edey. *Lucy The Beginnings of Humankind.* Simon and Schuster, 1981; Warner Books, New York, 1982.

Jordan, Francis, Jr. *Aboriginal Fishing Stations on the Coast of the Middle Atlantic States.* The New Era Printing Company, Lancaster, Penn., 1906.

Josephy, Alvin M., Jr., ed. *The American Heritage Book of Indians.* American Heritage, 1961.

Josselyn, John. "An Account of Two Voyages to New England." *Massachusetts Historical Society* 3 (1833): 211–354.

Kent, Barry C. *Susquehanna's Indians.* The Pennsylvania Historical and Museum Commission, Harrisburg, 1989.

Keppler, Joseph. "The Peace Tomahawk Algonkian Wampum." *Indian Notes* 6 (1929): 130–38.

King, J.C.H. *Thunderbird and Lightning.* British Museum Publications, Ltd., 1982.

Leakey, Richard, and Alan Walker. "Homo Erectus Unearthed." *National Geographic* 141, no. 3 (1972): 624–629.

Leland, Charles G. *The Algonquin Legends of New England; or, Myths and Folk Lore of the Micmac, Passamaquoddy, and Penobscot Tribes.* Houghton, Mifflin and Company, Boston, 1884.

MacGowan, Kenneth, and Hester A. Joseph, Jr. *Early Man in the New World.* Doubleday, Garden City, N.J., 1962.

MacNeish, R.S., Cunnar, G., Jessop, G., and P. Wilner. "1993 A Summary of Paleo-Indian Discoveries in Pendejo Cave Near Orogrande, NM." The Annual Report of AFAR for 1993, Andover, MA.

McCutchen, David. *The Red Record: The Oldest Native North American History.* Avery Publishing Group, Inc., New York, 1989.

McDonald, Jerry N., and Susan L. Woodward. *Indian Mounds of the Atlantic Coast.* McDonald & Woodward, Newark, Ohio, 1987.

Manakee, Harold R. *Indians of Early Maryland.* Garamond/Pridemark Press, Baltimore, 1981.

Miles, Charles. *Indian and Eskimo Artifacts of North America.* Bonanza Books, New York, 1968.

Montagu, Ashley. *Man His First Two Million Years.* Columbia University Press, New York and London, 1969.

Newcomb, William W., Jr. *North American Indians: An Anthropological Perspective.* Goodyear Publishing, Pacific Palisades, Calif., 1974.

Peterson, Harold L. *American Indian Tomahawks.* Museum of the American Indian, 1965.

Pfeiffer, John E. *The Search for Early Man.* American Heritage, New York, 1963.

Pollard, John Garland. *The Pamunkey Indians of Virginia.* Smithsonian Institution, Bureau of Ethnology. Washington Government Printing Office, 1894.

Rippeteau, Bruce E. "The Upper Susquehanna Valley Iroquois: An Iroquoian Enigma." *Occasional Publications in Northeastern Anthropology,* No. 5 (1978): 123–51.

Ritchie, William A. *The Archaeology of New York State.* The Natural History Press, Garden City, N.J., 1965.

Robinson, Donald, photographer. *Arrowhead Flaking Techniques at Plimoth Plantation.* Plimoth Plantation, 1963.

Russell, Howard S. *Indian New England Before the Mayflower.* University Press of New England, Hanover, N.H., 1980.

Silverberg, Robert. *Mound Builders of Ancient America.* New York Graphic Society, Greenwich, Conn., 1968.

Simmons, William Scranton. *Cutantowwit's House.* Brown University Press, Providence, 1970.

Skinner, Alan. "An Old Seneca Warclub." *Indian Notes* 3, no. 1 (1926): 45–47.

Snow, Dean R. *The Archaeology of New England.* Harcourt Brace Jovanovich, New York, 1993.

———. *The Archaeology of North America.* Viking, New York, 1976.

Speck, Frank G. "Northern Elements In Iroquois and New England Art." *Indian Notes* 2, no. 1 (1925): 1–12.

Spiess, Mathias. "Connecticut Circa 1625: Its Indian Trails, Villages and Sachemdoms." Edited by Elinor Ingersoll. Colonial Dames of America, 1934.

Stewart, T.D. *The People of America.* Charles Scribner's Sons, New York, 1973.

Stuart, George E., and Gene S. Stuart. *Discovering Man's Past in the Americas.* National Geographic Society, Washington, 1969.

Trigger, Bruce G., ed. *Handbook of the North American Indians.* Smithsonian Institution, Washington, 1978.

Trinkaus, Eric, and Pat Shipman. *The Neanderthals: Changing the Image of Mankind.* Alfred A. Knopf,

New York, 1993.

Turbyfill, Charles O. "Steatite Effigy Pipe from the Old Cherokee Country in North Carolina." *Indian Notes* 5 (1928): 318–321.

Wallace, Paul, A. W. *Indians In Pennsylvania*. The Pennsylvania Historical and Museum Commission, Harrisburg, 1991.

Walthall, John A., *Prehistoric Indians of the Southeast*. University of Alabama Press, Tuscaloosa, 1990.

Waring, A. J., Jr., and Preston Holder. "A Prehistoric Ceremonial Complex in the Southeastern United States." *American Anthropologist* 47, no. 1 (1945): 1–34.

Weaver, Kenneth F. "The Search for Our Ancestors." *National Geographic* 168, no. 5 (1985): 561–623.

Whitehead, Ruth Holmes. *Micmac Material Culture from 1600 A.D. to the Present*. The Nova Scotia Museum, Halifax, 1980.

Wilbur, C. Keith. *The New England Indians*. The Globe Pequot Press, Old Saybrook, Conn., 1978.

———. *Indian Handcrafts*. The Globe Pequot Press, Old Saybrook, Conn., 1990.

———. *Early Explorers of North America*. The Globe Pequot Press, Old Saybrook, Conn., 1989.

Wiley, Gordon R. *An Introduction to American Archaeology*. Prentice Hall, New Jersey, 1966.

Williams, Roger. *A Key into the Language of America* (London, 1643). Fifth edition reprinted at Providence for the Rhode Island and Providence Plantations Tercentenary Committee, Inc., 1936.

Willoughby, Charles C. "Antler-Pointed Arrows of the Southeastern Indians." *American Anthropologist 3* (1901): 431–37.

———. *Antiques of the New England Indians*. Harvard University, 1935.

———. "Prehistoric Workshops at Mt. Kineo, Maine." *The American Naturalist* 35, no. 411: 213–19.

Wissler, Clark. *Indian Costumes in the United States*. American Museum of Natural History, New York, 1926.

Wood, William. *New England's Prospect* (London, 1634). Edited by Alden T. Vaughan, University of Massachusetts Press, Amherst, 1977.

Woodward, Arthur. "The Metal Tomahawk Its Evolution and Distribution in North America." *The Bulletin of the Fort Ticonderoga Museum*, 7, no. 3 (1946).

Woodward, Susan L., and Jerry N. McDonald. *Indian Mounds of the Middle Ohio Valley*. McDonald & Woodward, Blacksburg, Va., 1986.

INDEX

Numbers appearing in **boldface** indicate illustrations.

ABOUT THE AUTHOR

A retired medical doctor who served as a naval officer in World War II, Keith Wilbur has written Globe Pequot's Illustrated Living History Series, which, with the addition of *The Woodland Indians*, now comprises nine titles. His abiding interest in our region's history has resulted in years of research for which he has traveled thousands of miles. While researching this title, Dr. Wilbur studied archives and artifacts at, among other places, the British Museum in London, England.